THE BUSINESS CASE ROADMAP – BCR:

from the idea to the business case

THE BUSINESS CASE ROADMAP – BCR:
from the idea to the business case

2018

Susana Costa Silva
Vitor Verdelho Vieira

ACTUAL

TÍTULO:
The business case roadmap – BCR: from the idea to the business case

AUTORES
Susana Costa Silva e Vitor Verdelho Vieira

CONJUNTURA ACTUAL EDITORA
Sede: Rua Fernandes Tomás, 76-80, 3000-167 Coimbra
Delegação: Avenida Engenheiro Arantes e Oliveira, 11 – 3° C – 1900-221 Lisboa - Portugal
www.actualeditora.pt

CAPA
FBA

PAGINAÇÃO
João Félix – Artes Gráficas

IMPRESSÃO E ACABAMENTO:
Artipol, Artes Gráficas, Lda

outubro 2018

DEPÓSITO LEGAL
447174/18

ACTUAL | GRUPOALMEDINA

BIBLIOTECA NACIONAL DE PORTUGAL – CATALOGAÇÃO NA PUBLICAÇÃO
SILVA, Susana Costa e, e outro

The business case roadmap – BCR: from the idea to the business case / Susana Costa e Silva, Vítor Verdelho Vieira. – (Fora de coleção)
ISBN 978-989-694-306-6

I – VIEIRA, Vítor Verdelho

CDU 005

We would like to thank Sara Mieiro Santos for the graphic design and Erica Prendeville for the proofreading.

Those of us associated not just with teaching matters related to entrepreneurship but, mainly, who have had the privilege of following closely the process of business creation, have encountered two related problems: 1) lack of materials that bridge theory and practice; 2) lack of literacy among potential entrepreneurs for building an adequately grounded business case. As in many other situations, seeing is believing. In the particular circumstance of entrepreneurship that means being able to clearly address the theory and models and being able to lead the reader to find situations that bear some resemblance with the one he has in mind or, perhaps, experiencing. This is a daunting task requiring the collection not just of a large number of examples, but also sufficiently diverse to allow useful illustrations.

Building on the experience and, in a sense, the complementarity of the authors' careers this book, and actually the series it inaugurates, is perhaps the best attempt, so far, to address the challenges sketched above. Built upon sound theoretical foundations – after all, there is nothing more practical than a good theory – enriched with multiple actual examples it will be a very useful tool for teachers, students and practioners.

Alberto Castro
Professor of Practice
Católica Porto Business School

Entrepreneurship – and being an entrepreneur – is nowadays fashionable and an activity seen in a very positive light. There has been, especially in the last decade – and fortunately – a very important process of social legitimation of the entrepreneurial activity. Even though historically it has always existed, during most of the time the culture of jobs for life, stability of employment, and less volatility of the labout market than it exists nowadays (with the change in business models, technologies, lifestyles) induced a status quo that somehow prevented a high percentage of very bright professionals from enterprising. Nowadays, with the development of entrepreneurial ecosystems all over the world, with the growing number of startups and accompanying organizations (incubators, accelaration programs, venture capital funds, a varied array of supportive public policies), with enabling technologies helping also in the process, and several relevant cultural changes, being an entrepreneur is a professional choice that is more and more desired and even aspirational. This is indeed very positive. And spans different generations, sectors and geographies. Governments now scramble to label themselves as startup nations, entrepreneurial states and the like.

However, how many cases of entrepreneurial ventures represent extraordinary ideas that go down the drain due to lack of method, of a professional approach, of an adequate team to implement the process, of inability to evaluate and reach relevant markets, of the most varied execution problems? Of asking the right questions at the beginning – and for that matter, at all phases – of the project?

Many.

Failing is part of the process and a learning opportunity, there's no doubt. But how many projects could embark on a brighter path if only the right questions were asked, if only a sound method and process-based approach was followed?

Here relies the importance of this set of three volumes. They are an invaluable help to any entrepreneur, with a very clear and pragmatic approach to all stages of the entrepreneurial act – from understanding the motivations to develop a project, from generating the idea, to executing and fully growing and expanding the project. Offering a tool-based approach, a systematic way of thinking and acting. And represents such a powerful added value to all entrepreneurs that read it.

"Business Case Roadmap" (BCR) is thus a timely and very welcome contribution to understanding – and, even better, implementing – an overall approach to business development. These three volumes cover all relevant stages: (i) from the idea to the business case; (ii) the implementation of the business case, addressing the execution challenge; (iii) the expansion of the business.

Framing very practically the issues, exploring the concepts, proposing a very intuitive and clear process and roadmap to navigate all phases of a project's lifecycle; dismantling clichés and asking what should be asked at all stages.

There's no doubt that the authors are very knowledgeable about the topics covered, representing a good balance and complementarity of academic depth and entrepreneurial experience, and through these volumes provide an excellent guide to all interested in setting up and growing a business.

As a policy-maker, I recognize an immense value in the approach followed by this collection of complementary volumes and by the systematic methodology proposed, in favour of all entrepreneurs and of the probability of success of all projects that benefit from the insights of these three volumes.

Ana Teresa Lehmann
State Secretary for Industry
XXI Portuguese Government

I have been teaching Entrepreneurship related topics since 1993, and at the time many gaps remained with regards to teaching materials and textbooks in the field. In the forthcoming two decades I was glad to see how the topic did become much more spoken and popular. As Is usually the case when this happens, lots and lots of different literature was then published and made available across the world, including many textbooks and multimedia contents. Although many of such references are quite useful, and I have been indeed using some of them, there was also a trend towards writing about Entrepreneurship in a rather superficial way, along the lines of "self-help" books, or based upon somewhat anecdotal evidence to support rather broad but unjustified recommendations or conclusions, sold under appealing book covers with somewhat disappointing pages inside. This "popularity" of Entrepreneurship ended up sometimes sending the wrong messages, like the notion that it is just and only a matter of attitude (which is a rather important but not the sole piece of the entrepreneurial journeys) or doable just by wishful thinking. Such a large variety of books, mostly written in English, contributed to my own decision, of just writing a book about Entrepreneuship after having over 20 years of experience of teaching and practice, and to do so in Portuguese and going deeper into the subjects, thus leading to a recent third edition having almost 700 pages...

This being the context under which I look into Entrepreneurship teaching and learning, I am really thrilled with the work accomplished by Vitor and Susana in putting together their Business Case Roadmap (BCR) trilogy of books. Along the lines of what I do believe in, and the perspective also shared by Bill Aulet (under his so-called Disciplined Entrepreneurship framework), the authors provide the readers with a wonderful journey about how to make Entrepreneurship happen, according to a vey well structured step by step approach. This set of three books is on one hand very practical, but also based upon a deep understanding of the subject, only possible due to the fact that both authors have a strong academic and scientific background, but they combined with extensive interactions and experiences on how to do it in real life scenarios and with hands on learnings collected over hundreds of entrepreneurial projects (I am very proud to have been one of the founders of NECTON, a biotechnology microalgae startup, back in 1997, under the leadership of Vitor, this being one of such cases). Such a combination resulted in a set of books that was clearly missing on the market and provides a very rich contribution to all people interested in studying, teaching or learning about Entrepreneurship in a rather evidence based and deeply supported basis.

The BCR trilogy of books does cover the full life cycle of entrepreneurial projects in a very consistent and well-structured approach, with step by step hints, tools and recommendations for each stage across this life cycle. The first stage corresponds to moving from a fuzzy idea to a well-supported business case. Although this is a critical process, nothing will happen unless we then move from the business case definition and planning to its real-life implementation and execution, which corresponds to the second volume. Finally, deciding what and how to move on, further develop the project, manage its growth and acceleration, corresponds to a not less important topic, covered in detail by the third book that completes this BCR collection.

Many congratulations to Vitor and Susana. They were able to put together a set of books that provides clear added value to the communities of people across the world that really want to learn more about Entrepreneurhsip, rather than just use the concept as a buzzword. The set of three BCR books, although based upon rather deep thoughts and lots of theoretical as well as practical experience, is also quite easy to read, follow and understand. I am pretty sure that it does cover one of the few gaps that remained in the literature about Entrepreneurship by 2019, as opposed to the many ones that I did find out to exist back in 1993... I strongly recommend that you pay due attention to this wonderful contribution, which I found worthwhile reading, keeping for future reference, that I truly enjoyed reading, and from which I did learn a lot as well. I am pretty sure that you will have similar thoughts and feelings after you have a chance of going through the wonderful materials provided by Vitor and Susana under this collection of Business Case Roadmap books.

Pedro Manuel Saraiva
Dean of NOVA Information Management School
Universidade Nova de Lisboa

What to expect?

Dear Reader, before we start we would like to inform you about what your expectations should be, as regards the contents of this book. At a time when being a entrepreneur seems to be popular, one might be tempted to think this means the conditions are right to succeed professionally. However, that is not always the case. Many people dream of starting a business, but only some actually achieve success.

We believe that every person has a certain level of inherent entrepreneurship. However, this shows itself in varying degrees and in different contexts. Not everyone is made to be a typical entrepreneur — and not all businesses that entrepreneurs start are destined for success. In the process of turning a passion or an idea into a great business, there are guidelines that ought to be followed, and expectations that need to be managed. This is also what this book is about.

It is *not possible* to teach you *how to be* an entrepreneur. However you can learn how to become a better entrepreneur. The entrepreneur's attitude is something that it is possible to develop and consolidate with knowledge and skills, even though it is *not* possible to obtain in a learning course.

It *is* possible to learn business development exclusively by analogy, using examples and case studies, but that has very limited results. Premature conclusions or incorrect validation procedures can lead to a misleading outcome. Furthermore, the absence of validation, when ideas are consolidated, can also lead to a global failure. A second and third opinion or mentoring are best practices. This is also what this book is about.

It *is* possible to have a sustainable business without a team, where leadership and multiple skills are centered on a single person. However, this would be a very unlikely scenario. Developing a business is not the same as developing a business idea. Execution is very different to ideation and requires different resources. Resources and a good team are both absolutely necessary. As a matter of fact, the Team is the most important factor for success and the 'Business Case Roadmap' (BCR) is centered on this concept.

What is this book about?

The 'BUSINESS CASE roadmap' (The BCR) collection presents a step-by-step procedure to find possible paths for the establishment of a business. *The roadmap follows an algorithm that is based on a logical sequence of operations, according to heuristic concepts and best practices.* People often have good business ideas and, in several cases, they follow them to start testing a business. This has proven to be the wrong approach when – for instance – the wrong questions are asked in a market survey. This can result in the idea being killed off before it has a chance to be developed. There is a wide range of possible paths which an idea can lead to. However, some are better than others, and some are even potentially destructive. Chance frequently plays an important role in the choice of paths, but relying on chance can lead to uncertain results, which we would like to avoid. We have based the construction of this tool on best practice methods observed over many years of experience in conducting business.

Each idea and each business team can follow an algorithm with a specific path or roadmap, based on a global sequence of interrelated steps, which can vary from business to business. This roadmap should be considered with a clear understanding of the different alternatives available. New business set-ups, existing business development or franchising can all follow the BCR. Hence, this process is useful in a variety of situations and has a wide scope.

The BCR is not an academic approach, but rather, a collated aggregation of entrepreneurs' visions, based on their knowledge and experience. Key concepts and definitions are used to simplify complex topics, and facilitate the understanding and use of concepts that represent the state-of-the-art in business development. We believe that following the proposed algorithm will lead to the highest predictable chances of success.

About the authors

Who are we?

Vitor Verdelho Vieira is mentor of several companies that he co-founded with partners in different sectors. He started his first biotech company – Necton, SA (www.necton.pt) – in March 1989, and it is now a European leader in the production and sale of traditional sea salt and *fleur de sel*, as well as the production of microalgae for aquaculture and cosmetics. He is also co-founder of A4F – Algae for Future, SA (www.a4f.pt) – an international reference company in the sector of microalgae technologies. He is the President of EABA, the European Algae Biomass Association, which has its headquarters in Florence. His business experience is wide and ranges from engineering consulting and real estate to biotechnology and medical devices. Within these different companies, he has developed and participated in more than 40 R&D projects over the last 25 years and interacted with more than 200 different organizations in Europe. From 2000 to 2015 he was involved in the management of SpinLogic, an entrepreneurship programme and business incubator at the Universidade Católica Portuguesa in Porto, during which time he followed and supported more than 150 projects. He is presently visiting professor at Católica Porto Business School, and the School of Arts at the same University. He has a background in Physics from the University of Porto and established his management knowledge via more than a dozen specialized training courses in Portugal and abroad over the last 30 years. https://pt.linkedin.com/in/vitorverdelho

Susana Costa e Silva has a Ph.D. in Marketing from University College, Dublin (Ireland), a MSc. in Economics from the University of Porto and graduated in Management at the Universidade Católica Portuguesa. She has been a lecturer at Católica Porto Business School (CPBS) since 1997. She has been the coordinator of the MSc. in Marketing and Management at CPBS, Researcher at CEGE (Research Centre in Management and Economics) and Member of CEGEA (Research Center in Management and Applied Economics). Over the years she has supervised more than 100 theses. Susana has authored several books and book chapters published in Portugal, the UK, USA and Brazil in the fields of Marketing and International Marketing, cooperation and alliances. She has presented her academic research at international conferences in the fields of Marketing, consumer behavior and international business. Her papers are published in international journals in the same fields. Susana is also active as a consultant in Marketing and International Business. She writes regularly for Portuguese magazines and newspapers. She is visiting scholar at universities in Brazil, China and Poland. She is also the national representative for Portugal at the European International Business Academy: www.porto.ucp.pt/feg/docentes/ssilva.htm?lang=1

What are our motivations?

We want to transform our combined knowledge and experience – which result from a diverse set of sources – into a useful tool that can be used by entrepreneurs, managers and business students alike. Throughout the years we have had direct access to more than 300 new businesses, and have studied and surveyed a further 300 on paper. We have found it useful to present our views on the analysis conducted over the years and systematize relevant insights from it into a series of 'best practices', in a compact and very straightforward way.

Using 'question and answer' methodology, we have been able to establish an algorithm that can be used to develop a 'Business Case'. This has been validated and tested by a wide number of MBA students and entrepreneurs. On the basis of this validation we have found our approach to be effective and innovative, providing an easy and fast learning process.

The BUSINESS CASE ROADMAP aims to set out a guided learning process, suggesting tools and clues which can be used for deeper exploratory work, and providing an interpretation of examples and case studies. Each individual and each team can benefit from this book differently; each person will have a specific topic and relevant examples to evaluate, and will develop a different interpretation of the arguments provided.

Dubitando, dubitando ad veritatem pervenimus...
[Famous sentence from Cicero that inspired Descartes]

Table of contents

Introduction 29
Why an algorithmic logic? 31

1. What are the different options for starting a business? 33
2. How to choose between starting a new business or developing an existing one? 39
3. What are the motivations for developing a business? 45
4. How to define 'the' business idea? 53
5. What is a 'Big Idea', and how to find a good business idea for me? 61
6. Where are the business opportunities, and how to find them? 69
7. What are the key success factors in the execution of a business? 77
8. How to find a Team to develop a business idea? 81
9. How to validate the business idea? 91
10. What is a Business Model? And how to develop one? 99
11. Wich is the best business model for my idea? 107
12. How to evaluate the Market? 115
13. How to differentiate from competitors? 121
14. What are the motivations and processes for innovation? 127
15. How to innovate in the process of business development? 133
16. What is a Business Case? How does it compare with a Business Plan? 139

17. How is a Business Case structured? 145
18. How to present a Business Case? 151
19. How to develop and implement the Business Case? 157
20. What is the role of the Business Case in transforming Ideas into Business? 163
21. Concluding remarks and Key ideas 169

Vol. 2

The BCR – how to implement the Business Case: the execution

Vol. 3

The BCR – how to expand the Business Case for business growth

Introduction

The **Business Case Roadmap** presents a step-by-step procedure to establish a business, according to a logical sequence of operations based on best practice strategies and heuristic concepts. There is a wide range of possible options an entrepreneur may choose during the development of a business idea. Some of these are better than others – and some can even be destructive.

The level of success a business can expect is uncertain, and chance frequently plays a significant role. However, best practice methods can help to find the algorithm that works out the highest predictable chances of success for each business. Hence, each idea and each business team will be challenged to follow a specific path based on a global sequence of interrelated and variable steps. A new business set-up, the developing of an existing business or even a franchising model can all follow this algorithm.

We would like to highlight that the **Business Case Roadmap** is not an academic approach, but rather a collection of entrepreneurial visions, based on knowledge and experience. Key concepts and definitions will be used, to turn complex topics into simple ones, and to understand and use state-of-the-art concepts in business development. Sometimes the same concept is repeated along different frameworks.

The first volume in the collection describes the steps from the emergence of an idea, whatever that might be, to its transformation into a business idea, and its further development into a business case. A business idea is understood as being an idea that responds to a certain need, providing a transaction with added value to all parties involved.

The 'Business Case' is an operational tool, developed by the project team, which describes a set of statements and responds to the critical questions that define the business and its development. Typically a two-page document, it works as a summary of the execution of the business plan. It is a compact and flexible document that is shared by the team and that can be adapted step-by-step, as the business evolves and adjusts to the competitive environment and needs of the market. The business case is more a compact guide than a business plan but can be expanded to become a business plan, if required.

Why an algorithmic logic?

An algorithm "is a sequence of instructions telling us what to do"; algorithms are reducible to logical operations that can be inter-related. By using a 'question and answer' methodology, we can establish a possible algorithm for the development of a business case. Testing – by a large number of MBA students and entrepreneurs – has found this approach to be effective and innovative, providing an easier learning process. The specific questions represent the most common questions asked by students and by entrepreneurs starting new businesses. The answers are based on best practices and academic information regarding reference concepts and definitions.

Before starting the business development process, it is critical to understand why we have chosen the specific path and options that we have. When we do, the process flows in a logical and natural way.

The responses to questions such as Who? What? Why? When? Where? How? and How much? require a clear understanding of the business, and result in a effective way to communicate the project to anyone who has an interest in it. By following this method, we are exposed to a dichotomous way of thinking that can provide an easier set of options and the Business Case Roadmap pathway.

The dichotomous thinking approach is a simplified way to set apart the different options. There are always several possible options and potential paths to follow. It is critical to know in advance what the options are, and why they should be evaluated, so that it is possible to choose the one considered the best for the specific context of the team, resources and timing. The ability to create dichotomy greatly smoothes the process.

Validation is mandatory, but if done without previous development and appropriate tools, might kill the idea from start.

Many business fail for lack of validation and many ideas die due to incorrect validation. Often, validation is not done in the righ timming, loosing the momentum.

1

What are the different options for starting a business?

What should be the first decision when wishing to start a business?

There are only two options when facing the challenge of starting a business: (1) *Starting a new business from scratch; and (2) Transforming an existing business*. Both options have advantages and disadvantages and depend on the specific context. In each of these two cases, there are several types of business, from 'informal business' – where all responsibilities are centered on one person – to 'collective business', where different types of society are feasible. To start a new business it is not always necessary to start a new company. A new business may be set up within an existing company, and in some cases a business may even flourish without the existence of a company. As a matter of fact, businesses such as restaurants or consulting services may rely on just one person. However most businesses evolve to be companies with the inherent need to build up a legal entity carrying on a commercial or industrial enterprise. These provide reliability and responsibility to clients, suppliers and partners. Besides, if the business is considered within a company it can be traded, which would not happen if the business were in the hands of only one person.

What are characteristics of each business option?

	New business	Existing business
(+)	• Fresh start, new story, new life — new DNA • The business planning and idea ownership	• Already established — provides trustworthiness • Re-engineering of a business feels rewarding
(–)	• The reality shock of bureaucracy and costs • Absence of experience to break through the unknown	• Potential shadows or skeletons from the past • Proper due diligence is required to avoid surprises
(i)	• Creative *momentum* associated with the start • The 'birth feeling' of the entrepreneurs	• Possibility of synergies with previous businesses • Existing clients, partners and / or suppliers

What are the differences between the two options?

A new business created through the establishment of a new company is a process that always consumes time and money – even if in some countries it is possible to establish a company in under an hour, and with only a small amount of money.

Registrations and bank-related operations always require more time and 'mental space'. The critical factor for starting trading is the existence of a fiscal or VAT number.

A new business created using an existing company as a vehicle normally requires less time. Costs can be delayed, if agreed, and the legal writing – including fiscal issues – is assured from the word go. Branding and a legal change of activity code might be required. However that can be developed and obtained in just a few weeks, if the activity of the business is different to that of the initial one. Transforming, re-designing or re-engineering an existing business can be a very interesting approach. There are a large number of businesses that are inactive or have only marginal trading activity because in many instances they have difficulties taking off.

What will happen, whatever the decision is? Can we predict the future?

Regardless of the format or type of business, there are a limited number of possible paths. Therefore it is very important to know beforehand what options will be presented to the company during the course of its life. In fact, it is unavoidable that at a certain point companies will face one of three possible outcomes: (1) Remaining small – almost as a family business, maintaining the same size and passing from generation to generation, eventually dying out when there is a discontinuity in management; (2) Growing continually, and in the future merging or perhaps being acquired by a larger company, eventually dying during a sector or management crisis (in this case very large organizations can only survive while they remain adapted to the global environment); (3) Failing early, after a promising start (several studies show that more than 80% die in the first 7 years).

What is the business evolution life cycle? What does it look like?

The business evolution life cycle is simultaneously disappointing and a unique opportunity. It gives us the chance to understand what happens to most businesses, and to understand

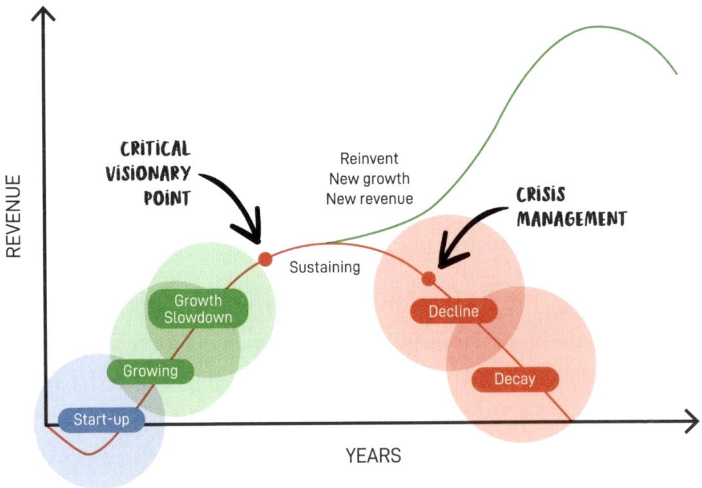

To buy or transform a business in decline can be a start-up option and an opportunity. Existing businesses can be refueled and re-designed with an injection of creative new ideas and dynamics. And this alternative may overcome some of the difficulties associated with the establishment of a new company. Indeed, everything about an existing business (apart from its age or start date) can be changed. A proper business 'story' can be developed according to the situation, using history to build value.
Source: adapted from: www.tomi.co.za/why-do-companies-follow-the-life-cycle/ accessed in 2018 Jan 20

that there are a large number of firms in either a situation of decline or of re-invention. Indeed, business activities are no different from anything else in the universe in this respect, and this knowledge can also provide an opportunity; their destiny can be anticipated and opportunities for re-invented business can be considered.

What are the options for transforming an existing business?

It is possible to transform a existing company to develop a new business using just its existing legal structure; it is possible to use a existing business and benefit from its corporate footprint. When starting a business using an existing company, the alternatives can be presented as follows:

<table>
<tr><td>New business</td><td>Develop a business from scratch</td><td>Start-up logics</td></tr>
<tr><td rowspan="4">Existing business</td><td rowspan="2">Transform an existing business</td><td>Buy the shares of a business</td></tr>
<tr><td>Buy a brand from the business</td></tr>
<tr><td rowspan="2">Choose a franchising business format</td><td>A new franchise in the region</td></tr>
<tr><td>An existing franchise</td></tr>
</table>

Why it is interesting to consider a Franchising Business?

It is possible to start a new business (a new company in a specific location and with a specific purpose) based on an existing business. Rather than transforming an existing company, another option is to adopt an existing business model and therefore benefit from what already exists. Very few people have the natural ability or expertise to be efficient in all aspects of running a successful business (1-5% of adults in Europe, according to the Global Entrepreneurship Monitor in 2016). Franchise organizations offer a structure for launching, operating and growing a business. Indeed, the successful franchisor will deliver the entire framework around which the business is built. Franchisors usually provide comprehensive operations manuals and training programs for their franchise owners that cover marketing, operations, accounting, technology and other areas specific to the business model in question. Setting up a business following an existing format is no less entrepreneurial, as there will always be opportunities to strive to be creative within the existing framework.

KEY IDEAS AND REFERENCES FOR MORE INFORMATION

- consider the possible options to start a business from new, transform an existing business or set up a franchise
- understand the future evolution of any company and business: the transformation life cycle

[1] Gilkey, C. (2014). The Small Business Lifecycle. USA: ProductiveFlourishing.com [accessed in 2018 Jan. 20]

[2] Neonakis, N. (2013). The Franchise MBA: Mastering the 4 Essential Steps to Owning a Franchise. ISBN 13: 9781494778347

[4] The Global Entrepreneurship Monitor is the world's foremost study of entrepreneurship (2018) www.gemconsortium.org [accessed in 2018 Jan. 20]

2

How to choose between starting a new business or developing an existing one?

What are the criteria used to decide between the two options?

The criteria depend on the framework associated with the business characteristics: (1) the timing and related opportunity; (2) the business development team; and (3) the business idea itself. Very often entrepreneurs forget about the possibility of starting with the acquisition of, or partnership with, an existing business. This scenario is less common than the one in which a company starts a new business.

Most of the time the criteria on which the choice is based relate to (1) people's motivations for getting into a business process (*why* do I want to do this?); (2) the origin of the business opportunity (*who* wants to do it?); and (3) the nature of the opportunity (*what* is there to be done?). Answering these questions is the first step towards business development.

How do I find existing businesses that can be transformed?

There are two possibilities to consider: (1) search through declining business in the specific sector of activity in which you are interested, using broad assessment criteria: initially, close to your preferred location (both geographically, and in terms of business sector), and later, outside it (it is always possible to think globally and then hone in); and (2) consider options in other sectors and change or adapt the 'business objective' accordingly.

What are the criteria for finding existing business to transform?

The first step, regardless of the options taken and the framework of the decision, is to develop proper due diligence concerning the business and to define the main criteria for decision-making. Therefore, we can consider two alternative options: (1) using the existing business and performing some changes in the business model; or (2) using the legal framework of the existing business but changing the business completely. Regardless of the choice, the most relevant criteria for your decision is the 'freedom to act'. This means that the legal framework should not dictate the business idea. On the contrary, it should be considered as an enabler and not a restricting factor.

How to find existing business that can be transformed?

The first thing to do is to define a profile of the target business, with a set of parameters concerning size, history and current situation (internally and externally). It is not an easy task but if we follow the dichotomous approach, there will be two basic global options:

Looking for it evaluating available information	Finding it advertising what you want
Search sector-related databases and other available data	Define a post and disseminate it through relevant locations
Ask your network contacts to search on your behalf	Establish a selection process for the data retrieved
Use your judgement to decide on the best options	Use your wider networking resources throughout the process

How to define the parameters for our options?

Faced with the first set of data available, other questions arise, for example: What are the most common choices? How should I decide? What would be the best criteria to use in the decision-making process? How do I know that I am making the correct decision? A fine tuning approach normally helps here. For instance, in order to narrow down the number of possible alternatives, we may use criteria to exclude some options. A good approach is one that minimises the 'gap' between the objectives we have defined and the attainment of the required results.

Why do entrepreneurs tend to prefer to start companies?

There are several reasons: (1) the first is that they assume that it is the only way to do it. In fact, most start-up programmes and initiatives suggest this as the only way; (2) then, we also have the ownership and the entrepreneurial drive to give birth to a business, the appealing idea of starting from scratch; and finally (3) it may be that there is no other opportunity and that starting anew is the only option.

The preference for starting companies is widespread throughout the world. Different countries and even regions show, over the years, different levels of new business drive, depending on background culture and educational policies and initiatives. The 'start-up call' often results from charming activities, such as boot camps, sandbox events and accelerators, as well as entrepreneurship competitions. These activities capture the attention of people who are attracted to these opportunities to shine, supported by public incentives, which abound in most countries.

Why do entrepreneurs avoid acquiring existing business?

We believe there are several reasons for this: (1) acquiring a small business tends to require more capital than creating a new one; (2) people don't know how to find the gems among existing businesses for sale (3) people want to introduce a particular product or type of enterprise they think is missing in the marketplace; (4) there is a feeling that a firm is the entrepreneur's 'baby', from which he is reluctant to detach himself (and we tend to see this as a feeling that may hinder further decisions regarding the project); (5) even though the acquisition of existing business is aligned with the 3 R's model (Reducing, Recycling, Re-using), resulting in less paperwork, fewer resources and less time, most people do not realize that.

Why is interesting to consider buying – or investing in developing – a new Brand?

There seems to be an increasing trend in recent years, of starting a business to test the business idea. This means we can create a brand supporting a business model – and only after this proves to have room for growth in the market, do we create the firm supporting it. As a matter of fact the registration and ownership of a brand does not require the creation of a company. A virtual company can be established online to validate the idea and create value associated with the brand. This is becoming a common option, not only because it reduces costs, but also because it is simpler, easier, generates value and can be expanded.

What are the main differences between Brand Development vs. Business Start-up?

Brands can be owned by individuals or by companies. Some people think that in order to develop a business it is necessary to create a company. However, that is not necessarily true. In fact many entrepreneurs often choose to create (or acquire) a brand which they use to name their business. The differences between developing a brand and creating a company to host a business exist essentially at two levels: (1) the registration and related accounting and (2) the associated legal responsibility. If an entrepreneur registers the brand, he/she has full individual responsibility and accountability for it. Corporate businesses are made up of a collection of people and therefore the responsibility is not an individual one.

Brand acquisition or development	**Company acquisition or management**
Brands may require a historical or impact evaluation	Requires proper due diligence to avoid negative surprises
Registration offers intellectual property protection	Must be properly registered with trade authorities
Full responsibility belongs to the person named on the brand registry	Responsibility level depends on type of company and country
Brands have intrinsic value related to reputation and awareness	Companies' value depends on the value of their client portfolio

KEY IDEAS AND REFERENCES FOR MORE INFORMATION

- the options on how to start are not decisive but will strongly influence the business development process and directions
- starting something completely new, developing a brand or establishing a franchising business are some of the options

[1] Howson, P. (2008). Checklists for Due Diligence. Surrey: Gower publishing ltd.

[2] Calkins, T. & Tybout, A. (Eds.). (2017). Kellogg on Branding: ISBN-13: 978-0471690160

3

What are the motivations for developing a business?

Why do entrepreneurs start a business? What are their main motivations?

Discussions with many entrepreneurs, and the evaluation of many start-up businesses, show there are three global drivers that normally attract entrepreneurs. These are also often referred to in books and articles about entrepreneurship and can be described as follows:

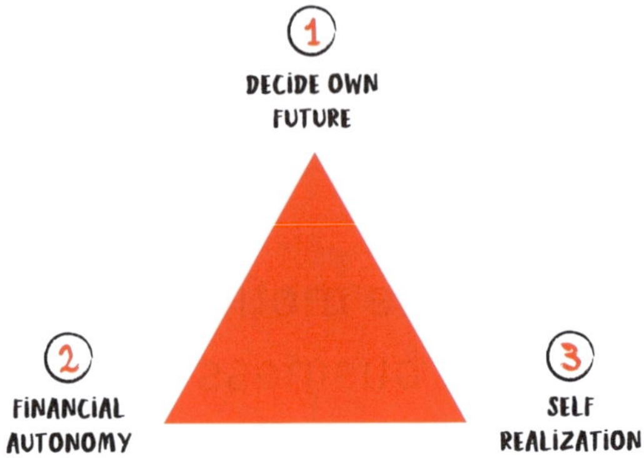

(1) the opportunity to decide their own future and have the associated flexibility and control over their work;

(2) the chance to obtain financial autonomy and gain results that are proportional or related to the level of effort put in;

(3) a way to achieve self-actualization which includes the chance to form a team and the feeling of a legacy.

How do the motivations to start a business originate?

Analysis of people's motivations to start a business shows that much depends on their perspective, which can be team driven or market driven. In fact it may be a team (either entrepreneurial or professional) that initiates the process. On the basis of their inner initiative they go to the market and look for opportunities. In other cases we may have latent opportunities that are identified by an existing team (again, either entrepreneurial or professional). In the first case an entrepreneurial team is more common whereas in the second, opportunities are mostly followed by professional teams. These professional teams within a company or other organization may start a business and develop a business case.

The motivation behind the firm's inception shapes its DNA: its unique combination of vision, mission and values. This is one of the main reasons why understanding the motivations behind starting a business is important: the more professional a team is, the more scrutinized the opportunities will be, and the more rational the process; the more entrepreneurial the process, the more innovative and emotional it will be.

Motivation to start a business			
Team-driven		Market-driven	
Entrepreneurial team	Professional team	Entrepreneurial team	Professional team

Why is it important to understand the motivations of the teams?

A business can be started by a team of entrepreneurs or by a team of professionals. Their motivations are different in each case. But in both cases they look for opportunities. Very often, starting a new business within an existing company is a corporate decision to explore an opportunity or to follow a visionary insight.

Motivations depending on who starts it	**Existing Opportunities**	**Latent Opportunities**
Entrepreneurial team	Disruptive innovation normally occurs	Typically opportunities in niche markets
Professional team	Typically developed by merger & acquisition	Typically opportunities developed through RDI (*)

(*) RDI – Research, Development and Innovation

What is the role of opportunities in starting a business?

The opportunity is often the triggering factor – the spark that ignites the latent wish or need to do it. Entrepreneurs perceive opportunities as being the driving force to move forward. **It is the combination of the strength of the motivation and the opportunity – including the *momentum* – which generates the overall business purpose.** Often the driving motivation of entrepreneurs is the realization of a vision that is supported by a potential opportunity. On the other hand, we may have a professional team just looking for opportunities to explore, such as legal gaps or a shortage of resources in a certain geographical area. Both cases lead to the development of new business. Sometimes, this process happens at the same time: exploration of an opportunity where both entrepreneurs and professional teams from firms act side by side, normally using different perspectives and different approaches to the same market need.

Why is the 'business motivation model' important?

The 'business motivation model' is the set of statements that defines the business and include its Mission, Vision, Values and Purpose. These business motivations are translated into a set of statements that support the integration of the different business drivers. Examples can help us to understand these concepts:

Source: adapted from Business Motivation Model – Object Management Group – www.omg.org [accessed on January 20, 2018]

What is a 'Business Mission'?

The mission describes what business the organization is in, both now and projecting into the future. Its aim is to provide focus for management and staff. A consulting firm might define its mission by the type of work it does, the clients it caters to, and the level of service it provides. Examples:

IKEA: To create a better everyday life for many people.

MICROSOFT: Empower people through great software anytime, anyplace, and on any device.

STARBUCKS: To inspire and nurture the human spirit – one person, one cup and one neighborhood at a time.

LENOVO: To become one of the world's best personal technology companies, which it is going to accomplish through product innovation, and better management.

What is a 'Business Vision'?

The Vision statement is supposed to state what the organization wishes to be like in some years' time. It defines the present ambition and unveils what will be in its timeline. Examples:

AMAZON: Our vision is to be Earth's most customer-centric company;

DISNEY: To make people happy.

GOOGLE: To organize the world's information and make it universally accessible and useful.

INSTAGRAM: Capture and Share the World's Moments.

LENOVO: Vision is that Lenovo will create personal devices more people are inspired to own, a culture more people aspire to join and an enduring, trusted business that is well respected around the world.

Values +	Vision =	Mission	Purpose
		= What we do	= Why we do it
= Desired culture	= Wishes to be	Operating a business	Sharing a dream
		Inspirational	Aspirational
		Creates 'buy-in'	Instills 'ownership'
		Provides focus	Fuel passion
Source (1)		Building a company	Building a community
		Laying bricks	Building cathedrals

Mission, Vision, Values and Purpose statements define the corporate DNA building blocks.

KEY IDEAS AND REFERENCES FOR MORE INFORMATION

- the business DNA is defined by the business model combined with the values, vision and mission statements
- the business development must be promoted considering both the strategy and the implementation or operation programme

[1] Kaplan, R. S., Norton, D.P & Barrows Jr. , E. A. (2008). Developing the Strategy: Vision, Value Gaps, and Analysis

[2] Baskin, K. (2011). Corporate DNA: Learning from Life. ISBN-13: 978-0750698443

4

How to define 'the' business idea?

What is a Business Idea?

A business idea is a concept that can be used to make money. To use a metaphor, think of idea as the base of a pyramid, on which the business will be built. Usually it centers on a product or service that can be offered for money. Every successful business started as someone's idea. Although a business idea has the potential to make money, it has no commercial value initially. There is a difference between an idea and business idea: Both are born in the creator's mind. However the business idea results in an exchange which has value for both parties involved. For value to be created it is necessary to have alignment between internal and external factors: the skills and resources of the team should be put forward to benefit from contextual circumstances within a specific *momentum*.

How do I come up with a business idea?

There are many possible ways to generate business ideas. Using the dichotomy approach it is possible to consider two alternatives in the process of business generation:

Start with the idea and then look for the team to implement	**Start with the team** and then develop an idea the team can implement
The early stages of business development and pre-business validation are of critical importance because it is when many business ideas shift focus or are abandoned. Adding rigor and discipline to your brainstorming and idea evaluation process will be more effective.	
• Build check-lists of potential customer types and related pricing models: Evaluate the opportunities where these lists overlap	• Pre-validate through the evaluation of the top ideas with real potential users, customers, or suppliers and > Clearly define what is the need you will satisfy with your business idea.

How to define the business idea?

The best way to define a business idea is through a 'statement'. This initial statement can evolve, and can be fine-tuned or crafted over a long period of time, but it should include a primary reference definition. It is an important starting point in the definition of business objectives. The statement should be based on the market need (what need is fulfilled by our product or service?) and must refer to what the value proposition is. The business definition statement is also a relevant way to get alignment and common understanding within the business team, and eventually, other stakeholders.

How to recognize what is a good business idea?

To be good, an idea should provide outputs that exceed the inputs. In this process all endowments should be considered: capital, labor and land, but also knowledge, networking and time. In the construction of the business idea it is important that value is passed on to customers in the form of reduced costs, extra benefits or even both: this is where value creation lies. A good business idea must create value for all parties involved.

How to characterize the quality of an idea?

To find out about the chances of a specific idea within a specific market and check its innovative content and feasibility, it is necessary to conduct a plausibility check for pre-validation. The more details that are listed, the more consistent the characterization will be. The plausibility test for a business idea can follow a check-list of criteria that should include the following:

Relevance	Innovation	Uniqueness	Focus	Profitability
It must fulfil actual or latent customers' needs or solve their problems	It refers to new products; features new processes	It is unlike anything else within one category; or it is very difficult to imitate	It should avoid being several things at the same time; or for the same locations	It should provide results, at least in the long run

How do I validate and develop my business idea?

The best way to develop and validate a business idea is through the development of deep **competitor benchmarking analysis**. There is a global understanding that the positioning of competition, regarding an opportunity, can be considered a relevant criteria of the merit of the idea. In fact, our understanding is that the idea must provide a response to a specific need and that several competitors must already exist and be willing to provide alternative solutions for the need identified. This would provide evidence that the market exists. This doesn't mean that there is no room for breakthrough innovation. However, the odds of that happening (except out of a large organization) are slim. So, the key seems to lie in filling opportunities in the market's fringes. This way, scrutinizing what competitors are doing well – and not so well – provides an important source of information about the market and about what prospective clients may want. We should not forget that the clients of our competitors will also be our potential clients. So, the way they are currently served is relevant. Valuable recommendations for the validation can be summarized as follows:

Must have in business idea validation	This validation helps in...
1. Settle on just one global business idea	Focusing
2. Validate your idea with others	Defining clients following unbiased opinions
3. Simulate execution	Understanding client needs
4. Find a large market....	Understanding the size of the market
5. Make it a must-have, not a nice-to-have.	Starting to work...

The business idea validation can also take the following cumulative approaches:

Should have in business idea validation	Which means...
Consider and evaluate the relevant markets	Defining the core target market
Note down your ideas and expand them with the team	Brainstorming
Carry out a competitive analysis	Looking especially for the ones that respond to the same need
Define the first sketch of the business model	Detail whether money will come from a b2b or b2c approach (or both)
Create/design/sketch your mockup and then test it	Testing the product on a sample
Extend the research to a market survey	Expanding the sample and the depth of the analysis

What is profiling and how to do it?

Profiling is very important for business development and is required both for clients and competitors. Client profiling corresponds to the definition of the 'average client' from an average 'set of clients' and it includes (1) demographic data; (2) geographical origin; (3) psychographic characteristics; (4) global motivational drivers; (5) motivational patterns for purchase; (6) economical or income level; (7) regularity of purchase. Including additional parameters, depending on the sector, and developing an info graphic set-up is good practice. Where they are, why they buy and how we can get to them are the global targets of profiling. This exercise can be adapted to competitors.

Profiling provides a good understanding about who the clients are and helps to design a customer centric strategy. A good way to start this process is to look for the clients of existing competitors. As a matter of fact, we should keep in mind that the different weaknesses of competitors are a direct source of opportunities for improving our business idea. Thus the level of satisfaction of our competitors' clients can be a starting point from which to put forward a business idea.

How to use competitor profiling for business validation?

One relevant factor in the validation of a business idea is to become a specialist in the field. Indeed, we should be an expert in the area where our product or service will be offered. Otherwise we will be just one undifferentiated player. Valuable recommendations for the validation can be developed from competitor profiling and competitive analysis – and summarized as follows:

1. Identify the competitors (all that provide a solution for the same need)
2. Describe the relevant competitors (the ones that serve the same need our product or service is addressing)
3. Define criteria to differentiate competitors (product, service, channels, relationship, reputation and price)
4. Compile all the measures to compare with the relevant competitors (benchmarking)
5. Develop surveillance schemes to monitor competitors

What to do when the idea is not yet mature?

Very often the entrepreneurs or project managers who want to develop business ideas are convinced that they have something, but there is still some part lacking, that requires more time to mature. It is true that there *are* situations in which ideas emerge in 'Eureka!' moments, but it is more common for ideas to require time to develop. In this case, the best practice is to develop a 'Master Plan', which will work as a 'buffering' set of opportunities that will be given extra thought before moving on.

What is a 'Master Plan' for business development?

A Master Plan is first of all a repository of all information that we have been able to collect over time about possible business ideas. It is a dynamic, long-term planning written document that provides a conceptual layout to guide future growth and development. It is akin to a folder where all documents are stored and organized. It includes different inputs such as:

Competitor analysis	Worldwide market analysis	Trends and risks evaluation
Information on concept validation	Criteria for market validation	Assessment of business potential

Master planning is about connecting the dots between different ideas and related business sectors related to our specific objectives – from which additional opportunities can result.

This approach is inspired by urban planning, and the overall idea is to first establish the 'big picture' concerning the business idea and then move inwards This document serves as an organized repository of business ideas and registers their evolution and associated background. It is good practice to divide it in two parts: (1) a diary for the timeline; (2) a mind map infographic summary. There is a wide range of OS software applications to develop mind maps.

KEY IDEAS AND REFERENCES FOR MORE INFORMATION

- a business idea is related to an opportunity either based on the market or based on the entrepreneur framework
- relevant opportunities are related to a specific need or solution for a problem that exists or could potentially exist

[1] Fishbein, M. (2014). Where Startup Ideas Come From: A Playbook for Generating Business Ideas. ISBN 1500815896

[2] Sedniev, A. (2016). The Business Idea Factory: A World-Class System for Creating Successful Business Ideas

[3] Buzan, T. (2006). The Ultimate Book of Mind Maps

5

What is a 'Big Idea', and how to find a good business idea for me?

What is the concept of a 'Big Idea'?

There is a myth that a good idea is enough to leverage a business. In fact, in some business accelerators the emphasis is placed entirely here: there is the belief that a good idea will pull in a good team. However ,that is not necessarily true. Good ideas always need to be backed up by a team to develop them further. In theory, individuals can do it, but that is not at all common, or indeed advisable; in practice, the individual will always be constrained by his/her time. So, what is contained within the concept of the "big idea"?

A 'big idea' is an idea for a business where the potential outputs are clearly higher than the obvious inputs. As referred to previously, a business idea encapsulates a profitable exchange between parties. The producer receives compensation in exchange for something of value that the client voluntarily pays for.

Adapted from: http://fundersandfounders.com/how-to-tell-a-successful-startup, accessed in 2018 Jan 25

SOME KEY DEFINITIONS:

business = trade = exchange
idea = the 5W1H methodology: why? who? what? when? where? how?
opportunity = occasion or *momentum*
client = the person/entity who pays = the origin of payment and who promotes an exchange
competitor = the one that provides a response to the same need
measure = comparison using a scale

don't forget: Businesses won't exist without **client(s)** in a specific opportunity framework **(*momentum*)**!

How to transform a business idea into a big idea?

When looking for what makes for a successful business, it is good practice to compare each firm with other companies, understand why they have been profitable, and compare each element of the business (or benchmark) with a similar company, over the same time frame. The key success factors are usually identified retrospectively. However, looking back at the past can provide a good source of insights for the future, if properly evaluated. Most of the time, a business idea can turn into a big idea if the team fulfils the criteria that turned out to be key in that business. Furthermore, it all starts with a good team, because a good team can change the idea and the business model and look for appropriate funding; thus, a good team is crucial not only for initial brainstorming but also for adaptations made during the process. A good team will also validate the timing or *momentum* for the business idea.

How to evaluate the strength of a business idea?

A good business idea is related to an opportunity. Finding a good opportunity requires screening several of them. And, for that to happen, we need to be open-minded and receptive to ideas that may or may not turn into business. This can happen in all sorts of circumstances, whether we are actively looking for ideas (alone or within the team) or when we least expect them. As a matter of fact, if you enjoy the field in which you work and you become a specialist in that field, the chances of this happening are higher. Thus we should develop all possible efforts, so that our team enjoys what they are doing and become specialists in our field of interest. 'Luck' happens when good preparation meets an opportunity.

The knowledge acquired in this process of evaluating business ideas must be blended with our own interpretation, and a certain level of adjustment may be necessary for each case. Identifying which business ideas have real commercial potential is one of the most difficult challenges in planning. The acid test of the process is the application of three possible criteria in the assessment of a business idea. These criteria are also good for comparing with other alternatives:

(1) Utility for the client	(2) Value created minus related cost	(3) Business model potential

How do I know if an idea is a good one for me or for my team?

At this stage of the process, we need to apply the criteria mentioned earlier, to the set of opportunities identified. In order to obtain a shortlist we must compare between the different opportunities. The team must be involved in this process. To rank the opportunities contained in the shortlist, rational criteria should be used as much as possible, and in this process, ascertaining a weight to each criterion is useful. It is essential to attribute a level of importance to each, and a ranking. Ranking allows a better understanding of the relevance of the success factors. The key success factors are based on retrospective information, but they can provide prospective insights if properly evaluated. There is always room for your intuition throughout the process, and indeed, this might prove decisive at the end of the process.

How can we learn from the successes and failures of others?

Learning from others' experience is normally faster and less expensive than simply learning by doing. Some business ideas look very good and some immediately attract investors, talent, and customers, while others fail. The main reason for this usually relates to the *momentum* and alignment with the business concepts and trends at a particular moment in time. It is possible to direct our search for business ideas in a way that will increase the odds of finding a good idea, if we follow criteria from the following five categories:

1. **Mission Alignment** – Does this project feel like a fit with who we are and what we do?
2. **Financial Appeal** – Does this project present an attractive financial opportunity?
3. **Mojo Alignment** – Is this project differentiation aligned with our core competencies and resources?
4. **Quality of the Market** – Is this a big enough, growing, exciting market opportunity?
5. **Quality of the Business Model** – Does this have an appealing model? Am I able to explain and explore it?

What are the critical ingredients for the definition of a good business idea?

Studies conducted with companies that succeeded – and those which failed – highlight factors that are very commonly cited in the explanation of success and failure respectively. Bill Gross is the founder of Idealab, a business incubator focused on new ideas. He founded a lot of startups, and incubated many others – and he got curious about why some succeeded and others failed. So he gathered data from hundreds of companies – his own and other people's – and ranked each company according to five key independent factors. He found the following success factors (presented in a TED Talk in 2015) [3]:

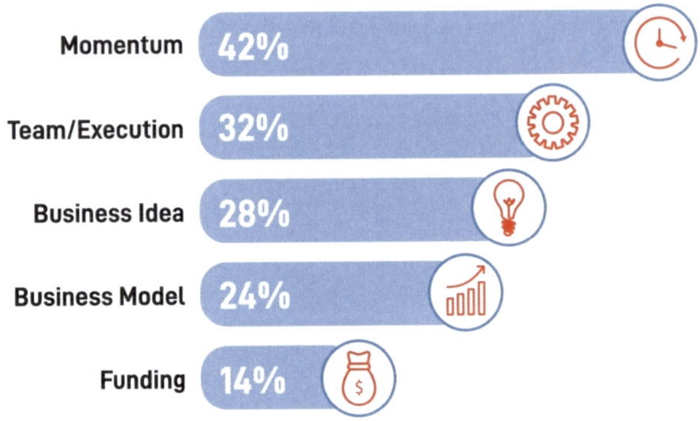

As we can see, the most relevant reason for success seems to be the time at which an idea was implemented, followed by the team. 'The idea' itself only comes third. The *momentum* of its implementation, and the time taken to do it, are pointed out by managers as more relevant. These factors refer to the question: 'What was more important to the success of each business?'

> ***MOMENTUM*** is critical, especially because we have no means of knowing exactly when to act. Often the moment to act is a matter of feeling and an 'educated guess', based on specific knowledge and experience that can be obtained from other business areas or contexts. We frequently see businesses launch 'out of time' – either ahead of, or after, the right time. To have the right idea, at the right time, and implemented in the right way, is key to success.

TEAM and **EXECUTION** are the central factors to any business in any field and at all times. The team is the global ultimate owner and factor for the success or failure of any human activity, regardless of whether this is business, sport or social activities. Without the team, the *momentum* is worthless, just as a team without the correct *momentum* will not succeed.
IDEA should be differentiated and supported by a strong 'value proposition'. The team, in a specific time frame of opportunity helps model the driving forces of the idea, and this may be fundamental for putting it forward. A good team will develop a good idea.
BUSINESS MODEL is how an organization creates, delivers, and captures value. There are many possible business models that can be adapted for each idea and business opportunity. Often several will work and several will lead to failure, but at any given moment in time and with any given team, there is one (or more) that provides the best results. In many business cases this is poorly defined.
FUNDING is the 'fuel for the engine' for a business and has several dimensions. This is strongly related to the business model.

KEY IDEAS AND REFERENCES FOR MORE INFORMATION

- a 'big' idea depends on a wide range of factors but the main constrain is related with necessary and available resources
- impact of ideas depends on the development team: a good idea for a specific team can be a bad idea for another team

[1] Kim, C. & Mauborgne, R. (0000). Knowing a Winning Business Idea When You See One. https://hbr.org/2000/09/knowing-a-winning-business-idea-when-you-see-one [accessed in 2018 Jan. 20]

[2] Yayici , E. (2013). Business Analyst's Mentor Book (2013)

[3] Adapted from http://video.ted.com/talk/podcast/2015U/None/BillGross_2015U-480p.mp4 [accessed in 2018 Jan. 20]

6

Where are the business opportunities, and how to find them?

What is a Business Opportunity?

A business opportunity is a proven concept that generates ongoing income. In other words, a business opportunity is a business idea that has been researched, refined and packaged into a promising venture that is ready to be launched. While multiple business ideas may strike you on a daily basis, only a few of them will be profitable in the long run, based on market research and feasibility studies conducted. These few are the real business opportunities and they must match the *momentum*. You can then either implement the idea on your own, or sell it to someone else for profit (perhaps because you cannot afford the capital required to launch the business). Selling a business opportunity is an alternative that is not always considered, but that can be a good solution for situations in which one or some of the necessary ingredients are not present. However if this is the case, the business opportunity needs to be well presented for the specific purpose.

What is the difference between a Business Idea and a Business Opportunity?

A major difference between an idea and an opportunity is that you can sell a business opportunity, but you cannot sell an idea (it is not entirely impossible but it is very difficult). Harland Sanders tried for many years to sell his chicken recipe idea, but no-one was interested. It was not until he repackaged it as a business, rather than a product, that KFC (Kentucky Fried Chicken) was born. The lesson here is that investors invest in business opportunities and ventures and not in business ideas. So, in order to be sold, an idea often needs to be dressed up with a business model and proven to be worth investing in. The business opportunity is timing- or *momentum*-related and is closer to implementation.

What are the main characteristics of a Business Opportunity?

An opportunity is regarded as being a good one after it has been found to meet several specific criteria that were collected on the basis of experience. A global check-list is often used, which ranks different levels of relevance and their related impact. The evaluation can be individual or collective, can lead to a 'yes' or 'no', or can compare different cases on a scale. As a matter of fact, many steering committees for startups use the following criteria to evaluate a business that they believe is a 'business opportunity':

Do the leading entrepreneurs and the team have the strengths and ability needed to drive the business to success?
Is the team's level of enthusiasm for the business credible and consistently very high?
Is the capital investment in the startup realistic and within the range of what you can provide?
Does the opportunity have the potential to make a residual income?
Does the opportunity give rise to a portfolio of offers rather than being based solely on a single product?
It must have gross margins above 20% in the case of most countries
It must have the potential to keep on improving as time goes by
It must have a low level of liability risk
It must have the potential to reach a break-even cash flow within 36 months on average

Where to look for business opportunities?

Gaining an understanding of the various 'sources' of business opportunities is complex and changes from team to team, as the recognition of opportunities depends on the sensitivity of the people involved, in relation to the sector. The challenge is often sensing opportunities. There are, however, four main conceptual 'places' where business opportunities usually pop up.

<table>
<tr><td colspan="2">Everywhere</td></tr>
<tr><td>Where needs are felt</td><td>Where best practices are consolidated</td></tr>
<tr><td>Where solutions for problems are found</td><td>Where borders or interfaces of sectors are located</td></tr>
<tr><td colspan="2">Combinations of different previous sources</td></tr>
</table>

Having an understanding of these 'places' will make it possible to focus, once a feeling or a impulse is felt by the entrepreneurs. For instance, a study of good practices at call centers gave rise to the development of web-based call centers. Similarly, people used the Web to search for feedback about hotel stays, so it was on the Web that some business models based on collecting consumers' reviews were created. Mobile fast food vans, for instance, are sub-divisions of fast food restaurants. Once we have a definition of a field of activity, based on background knowledge, an understanding of these four 'places' as opportunity generators can be very useful.

Additionally, opportunities can be sought in catalogs of business opportunities, for instance catalogs of franchising business models. Furthermore, it is necessary to follow an approach that considers additional sub-divisions within the same opportunity.

How to detect business opportunities related to existing and future needs?

Opportunities exist in all areas but to be able to better detect them it is crucial to have sensitive knowledge about the sector (i.e. be as much of a specialist as possible). The first step is to find the topic area , which should be related to the core competences of the team. Human need analysis, using the Maslow pyramid, is a possible framework for search and analysis. It can be used as a tool to help identify existing and future needs based on trend analysis.

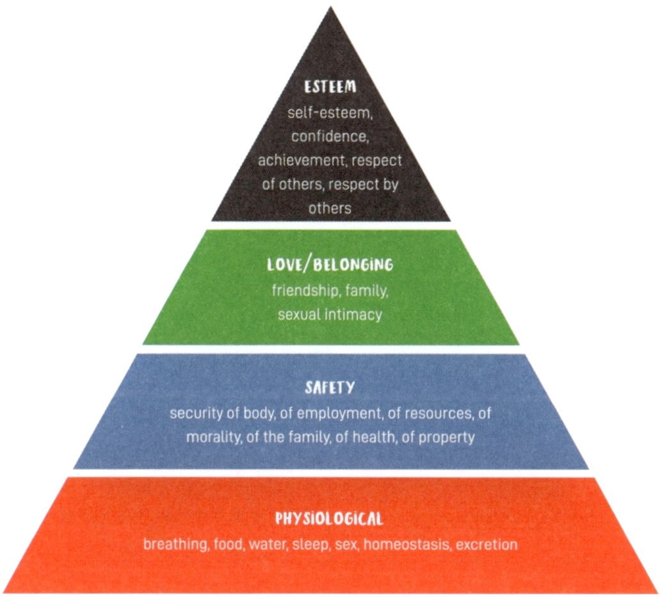

MASLOW'S HIERARCHY OF NEEDS

WHAT LEVEL OF NEEDS?

The needs of humans, as defined by Maslow in 1954, can be regarded as a good outlet to frame need to which value propositions may be addressed. However this classification of need is not absent of criticism – in particular, the idea that this ranking is not universal and therefore may vary across cultures due to individual differences and availability of resources in a particular region. Despite its anachronistic characteristics we still believe it is a good starting point from which to define our value proposition.

The Maslow pyramid is a reference concept to understand the global framework and hierarchy of needs. It is a starting point.

How to evaluate the business idea and the related business opportunities?

Each business framework will have a different best practice framework for analysis and evaluation. Ideally, the evaluation of business opportunities should be developed by the team, because this generates a sense of belonging and improves future commitment among team members. The process of detecting and evaluating business opportunities can progress according to the following stages:

First stage	Second stage (you can also start here)
Choose a sector of interest and become a specialist in that field	Define the sector that mobilizes your core competences
Study sector-related trends in reports	Develop a benchmarking study
Define a list of needs related to the trends	Talk with leading specialists in the field
Refine the previous steps and interconnect them	Build mind maps or use alternative methodologies
Move to the second stage	Brainstorm with the team using the information collected
	DECIDE

KEY IDEAS AND REFERENCES FOR MORE INFORMATION (please be inspired by these books!)

- Usually business opportunities do not fall from the sky, they need to be searched out actively or given attention
- To recognize a business opportunity is necessary to have a open mind and be prepared – opportunities are time critical

[1] Conley, C. (2007). Peak: How Great Companies Get Their Mojo from Maslow. ISBN: 978-0-787-98861-6

[2] Meisel, A. & Sonnenberg, N. (2016). Idea to Execution: How to Optimize, Automate, and Outsource Everything in Your Business. Lioncrest Publishing.

7

What are the key success factors in the execution of a business?

What must be done before execution?

Once there is a consolidated decision about the business opportunity, the next challenge is its execution. It is possible to turn a business idea into a business opportunity after conducting market research and a feasibility study on your idea, assembling a business team who will work with you on your idea, and writing a business case / business plan. It is only then that the idea will become an opportunity with the potential to attract investors and likely to get the necessary financing to thrive. Validation is critical and should not be simplified and underestimated. An understanding and oversight of the implementation challenges helps increase motivation and improve the validation process.

What areas should be covered in the execution?

It is generally understood in business development that there are several important areas for most businesses at the execution level. Concern about execution is very important in business development because at some point during the process of execution, there will be barriers or bottlenecks that often require a re-think of the business idea or a re-evaluation of the market. The following are some of the most relevant areas to consider:

A possible 'good practice is to create check-lists or mind maps to spot the critical areas that are 'sector sensitive'	
Strategic Focus	Leadership, Management, Planning
People	Personnel, Staff, Learning, Development
Operations	Processes, Work
Marketing	Customer Relations, Sales, Responsiveness
Finances	Assets, Facilities, Equipment

What are the main difficulties faced in the execution?

Analysis of many businesses has shown that most struggle with difficulties because the team members and leaders have an inadequate level of self-knowledge, and only discover their vocational strengths/weaknesses and procrastination areas when faced with real situations. The setting up of a complete team that covers the required areas of expertise is always very difficult and partnerships are sometimes developed to cope with that. Initially, partnerships may be very good. However, the team members' individual expectations may be difficult to meet. It is advisable that expectations are prioritized from the very beginning. Otherwise, difficulties can emerge that can put the business at risk. The key difficulties in the execution phase can be summarized as follows:

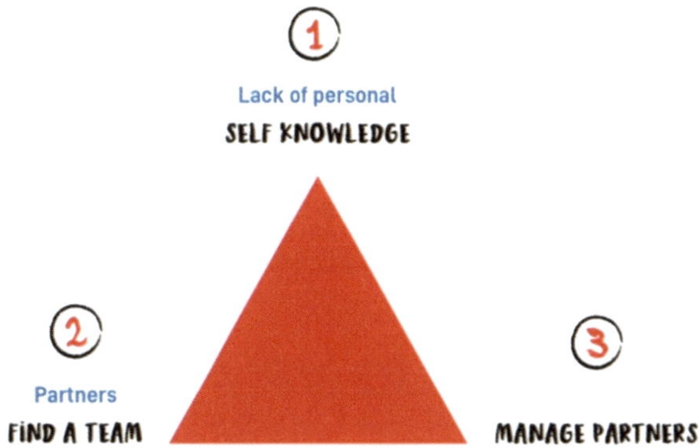

1. Lack of personal self-knowledge – very often the entrepreneurs do not devote time to knowing themselves and understanding their limits and skills;
2. Difficulties in finding partners for the team – usually the main complaint by entrepreneurs is that it is difficult to find partners for the team who can be trusted quickly.
3. Difficulties in managing partners' expectations – this is a difficulty that combines both the previous ones and adds external partners. It is usually is related to management of relationships.

KEY IDEAS AND REFERENCES FOR MORE INFORMATION

- business opportunities can be evaluated for a specific team and situation according to potential success factors
- once in possession of all possible relevant information, the most important decision making criteria for entrepreneurs is 'the feeling'

[1] Buck, E.W. (2011). The 5 Key Success Factors: A Powerful System For Total Business Success.

[2] Carroll, P & Mui, , C (2009). Billion Dollar Lessons: What You Can Learn from the Most Inexcusable Business Failures of the Last 25 Years.

8

How to find a Team to develop a business idea?

What is the concept of 'a Team'?

The idea of the 'business team' is very often the subject of several misleading interpretations. In fact, in most companies, the word *team* is used somewhat indiscriminately and almost interchangeably, referring to different things. For this reason, people management has become one of the most important disciplines in the learning of business development. It can, in fact, be considered in a wide range of contexts, but we need to disentangle those different contexts. Often they are not well separated, which generates business development problems. The following types of 'Team' levels must be considered:

(1) The **core team** – the one that is usually formed by all co-founders of the business	(2) The **overall team** – The team formed by all employees of the business sometimes referred as the staff	(3) The **task force team** – The team formed to pursue a certain project – typically with members of staff

What comes first: the (business) Team or the (business) Idea?

As we have already seen, often the process does not start with the idea, but rather with a team. Using the team as the starting point is as valid as starting with the idea. It is impossible to say that one way is better than the other, or that one way always happens first. However, there comes a time when the team should be the driving force. Team building and market validation are critical for business development. There are two levels to consider, because it is necessary to start with a 'core team', and only then begin to look for the 'extended team' or the people you can hire.

What are the steps to building the 'core team'?

There is no special way to build the 'core team'. It will be related to the framework, depending on questions like: What type of entrepreneurs? Where? When? Ikigai alignment (which we will discuss later in more detail) help provides a possible route to selection. There are also five relevant steps that are common and can be considered good practice in the process of building the 'core team' from the entrepreneur's point of view:

1. Define the characteristics (personal and technical profiles) you need;
2. Search your direct connections or the connections of people you trust;
3. Define a proposal that combines your offer and the potential interest of the possible team member;
4. Promote the connection; this should not be an interview but rather an exploratory and informal talk with a set of meetings, eventually alongside meals – and continue this until it is possible to decide whether there is a match. This is an important step and might require time, and eventually second opinions, from people you trust;
5. Integrate the new team member in a step-by-step process in which trust is being built. In this process, a close attention should be given to the management of expectations.

How to define the roles of people involved in the development of a business idea?

Entrepreneurs usually understand that the team should contain only people who are 100% dedicated. Often they identify relevant resources that they would like to attract, but those individuals are involved in other activities. However in some cases it is better to have some key people on the team in a part-time capacity, rather than involving someone – who doesn't bear the necessary skills – on a full time basis. Therefore it is important to identify the relevant people to involve in the project, regardless of the amount of time that they are able to commit to it. During this process it is advisable that roles and positions are well defined. Ideally each member of the team should be clear from the beginning about how much of their time, and which skills, need to be committed to the project. The duration of their involvement should also be known. It is not absolutely necessary to make all those who we regard as the right people members of the team. Some may be involved as members of a network.

What should be the role of the founders ?

The most important members of your team are the founders and/or providers of the 'business knowledge', which includes the business idea and related concepts. It is critical to have both the technical and the business or management skills. Before hiring anyone else (for the overall team), you and your co-founders (the core team) have to settle on how decisions will be made within the new business. For example, are you the technical expert and your co-founder the marketing partner? What will the different roles be within the core team? Only once this is defined is it possible to proceed with searching people for the rest of the team. At some point in the future, members of the overall team may become members of the core team.

What is the potential role of part-timers vs. full timers in the team?

There are two critical issues in the team development process. (1) The first concerns the dilemma of whether to have full-time members who are not an ideal fit or part-time members who are more ideally suited to the role. Then (2) there is the question of what type of contract it is appropriate to establish between employees with a higher level of commitment and contractors whose link to the business is not as strong. The answer to these questions will depend on the type of business and leadership. Some businesses require levels of confidentiality and IP protection which necessitate non-disclosure agreements or specific contracts. However, a mixed strategy is usually the best solution, as it is possible to make adjustments as the business evolves.

How to identify candidates?

The identification of people we want in our team is not an easy task. Ideally there are benchmarks for four areas of best practice that should assist in our decision: (1) Candidates should be in fields that are not currently covered: they have experience in areas that other team members do not. A common mistake is to have people from the same schools, with the same background and sometimes even of similar ages; (2) Candidates should be vouched for: you know them or know someone who knows them (the relevance of 'who knows who' asset is usually very important; they are endorsed or have references); (3) Candidates are able to start at a limited salary or for a compatible stake in the startup. It is important to be able to test them on the job and envision a process of evolution; (4) Candidates should be keen on your product / service or idea.

What is it important to know about the candidates?

A very important ingredient in the whole process is the alignment of the Ikigai of candidates with our own and also with the Ikigai of the rest of the team. If you can find people who meet similar Ikigai criteria, there is a great chance of putting together a winning team.

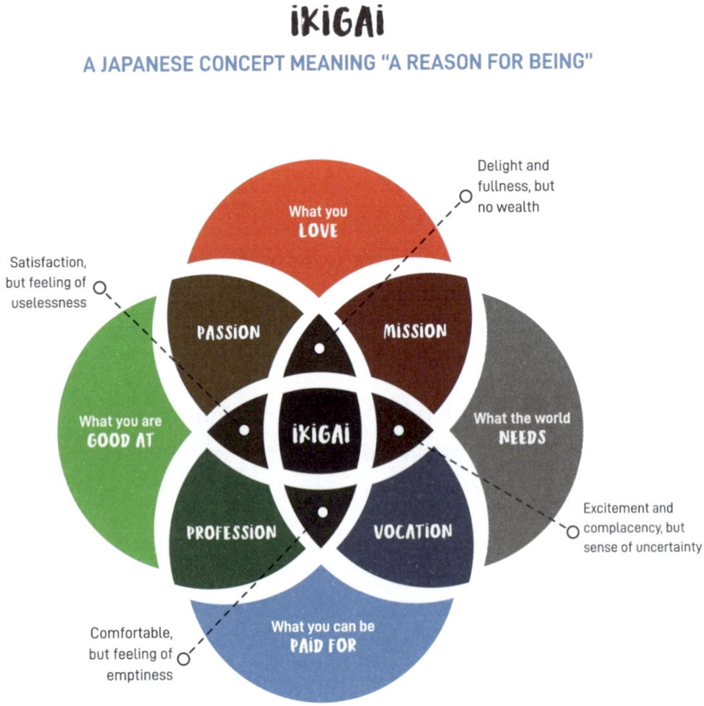

Ikigai-based people management is a 'best practice' method that helps to manage expectations and provides a better working environment. Source: https://barbarabray.net/2017/11/14/ikigai-your-purpose-and-reason-for-being/, consulted in 4/5/2018.

The World Economic Forum's 2018 report, The Future of Jobs, contains some fascinating research. In particular, the report asked chief human resources and strategy officers from leading global organizations to identify the skill sets the workforce of 2020 will need. Compared side by side to the skills identified as needed in 2015, the shifts aren't dramatic – except for one skill: creativity.

It will be good practice to look for the following skills which are considered by many experts as the the top 10 most relevant skills for 2020 employers: 1. complex problem solving; 2. critical thinking; 3. creativity; 4. people management; 5. teamwork; 6. emotional intelligence; 7 judgment and decision making; 8. service orientation; 9 negotiation; 10 cognitive flexibility.

How to develop the hiring process for the extended team?

After people have been qualified as candidates it is time to start the hiring process, which usually begins with an interview. Here, it is advisable to follow some recommendations:

1. Before the interview: have questions covering issues such as facts from the CV that can be confirmed (for instance: university of graduation, subjects taken, etc.), people's creativity (which can be demonstrated by, for example, people revealing their abilities to cook), their ability to solve problems (for instance, challenges accomplished in life), a candidate's ability to work in teams (for instance, ask them to recount situations in which this competence was demonstrated), and, finally, manifested behavior (for instance, understand if extremist positions are held; everyone is entitled to have them, but this can be a signal of attachment);

2. During the interview: Look out for nonverbal clues: be attentive to candidate's posture, body language, dress code. Create an agenda with questions.

3. After the interview, do some fact checking and a background check on the potential employee. We need to be able to confirm some of the information passed on during the interview.

It is good practice to carry out the hiring and integration of a person in the team as a staged process. Once the person has been considered, give him or her tests. Start with a smaller projects and work up to larger tasks. During these tests, you can see how the prospective employee communicates with other team members and handles pressure, and whether he or she can actually get the job done. If everything goes smoothly, it is time to go ahead and hire.

How to handle the post-hire period?

Post-hiring, it is critical to have information about the employee's Ikigai. Once that person has been hired, it is necessary to do some post-hire assessment. This means having strategies in place for training, promotion, and career development. Failure to do this will result in many problems in the future as there is a high chance that expectations will not be satisfied. These will also serve as an incentive and motivation. This is especially relevant for start-ups and new businesses where the effort and cost of the process of looking for a new team member are both very high.

IF YOU WANT
TO GO FAST,
GO ALONE.
IF YOU WANT
TO GO FAR,
GO TOGETHER.

- AFRICAN PROVERB -

KEY IDEAS AND REFERENCES FOR MORE INFORMATION

- references form potential team workers are critical because it is very difficult to know a person only with an interview
- trust is key factor to find in a team

[1] Hume, D. (2018) Building Great Startup Teams. ISBN-13: 978-1364293833

[2] Salgaller, M.L. (2010). Biotechnology Entrepreneurship from Science to Solutions – Start-Up, Company Formation and Organization, Team, Intellectual Property, Financing. ISBN-13: 978-1-934899-13-7

9

How to validate the business idea?

What are the best practical ways to validate a business idea?

This is one of the most important topics in business development and should be done by the core team. There is no magic formula. To validate the business idea we recommend analyzing three aspects: the product/service, the clients and the competitors. Thus, the validation checklist must include: (1) Revisiting the idea and understanding in detail what need is being satisfied by the product/service we are producing – confirm ing there is an alignment between the need and the product or service developed to fill that need; this must be extensively discussed by the core team; (2) Assessing existing and potential competitors (corporate and business information regarding each of the most relevant competitors), now that a better definition exists of the product/service at hand; competitors are those that provide answers to the same need, even if with different products or services; (3) Defining the prospective clients using profiling and related preliminary segmentation; Focusing on the information about how many units we believe they can buy and how much they would be willing to offer for the product/service. Client profiling, and understanding the related needs, provide a relevant support for validation.

Validation requires evaluation

We should be able to obtain information about our competitors' assortment of products and services, the level of prices charged, their business model and the clients they say they have. This approach will lead to a better understanding of the market opportunity and allows for the creation of the necessary support information to develop specific analysis to evaluate the idea. If it is difficult to find out who the direct competitors are, that may be a signal that there is no effective room for the business. However, some people tend to think that their idea is so innovative that there is no competition for it. This way, the "absence" of competition is usually interpreted as a good thing. Our own view is that it may be a signal that the need is not strong enough to position our product. However, we always recommend a more precise analysis which should include quantification of the market potential.

What is a PESTLE analysis and how to develop it?

In order to have a global vision regarding the business framework it is very important to consider external factors and areas of interface. One of the tools that can be used to look for information about the framework is the PESTLE analysis. The PESTLE – **P**olitical, **E**conomic, **S**ocial, **T**echnological, **L**egal and **E**nvironmental – analysis is a set of drivers to analyze the key factors influencing an organization from the external macro environment (big picture) in which a business operates. It is an evolution of 'Scanning the Business Environment' , proposed by Francis J. Aguilar (1967), who discussed 'ETPS' – a mnemonic for the four sectors of his taxonomy of the environment: Economic, Technical, Political, and Social. PEST gained popularity in the 80s and is now a reference tool that can have variations according to the type of business. The best way to develop a PESTLE is to do a web search of similar PEST or PESTLE analyses and consider the emulation of those results. Some examples can be described as follows:

Political	Economical	Social / Cultural	Technological	Legal	Environmental
Services Infrastructure Tax policy Regulation	Growth rate Inflation Labor costs Business cycle	Demography Education Cultural norms Income dis.	Emerging tech. Tech Transfer R&D Efforts Communications	Regional laws Law enforcement Court system	Resource management Energy availability Workforce health Climate change

What is the Lean Canvas?

The **Lean Canvas** is derived from the 'lean startup concept' developed by Eric Ries (http://theleanstartup.com), and is also inspired by the Business Model Canvas, developed by Alexander Osterwalder (https://strategyzer.com). We believe Osterwalder's Canvas is a very important tool, but rather more useful in a later stage of the process – business ideas development – than during the validation stage. So we will focus on that tool later; for now, we will use the Lean Canvas.

> **Lean Canvas** was proposed by Ash Maurya in 2012 following the Lean Startup spirit (Fast, Concise and Effective startup). It promises an actionable and entrepreneur-focused business planning process. It focuses on problems, solutions, key metrics and competitive advantages with the motto: **Love the problem.**
>
> Lean management seeks to eliminate any waste of time, effort or money by identifying each step in a business process and then revising or cutting out steps that do not create value. The philosophy has its roots in manufacturing but can be adapted and adjusted to any business.
>
> Guiding principles for lean management include:
>
> 1. Defining value from the standpoint of the end customer.
> 2. Identifying each step in a business process and eliminating those steps that do not create value.

3. Making the value-creating steps occur in tight sequence.
4. Repeating the first three steps on a continuous basis until all waste has been eliminated.

How to use the Lean Canvas as a simple validation tool?

To plot the proposed framework, we recommend starting with the identification of both the problem and the solution. Our view is that the definition of the need is paramount, as it allows us to find the problem and the inherent value proposition. The solution for the problem is the response to the problem, and the value proposition is the differentiated way we propose to generate revenues in the provision of the response to the identified need. The cost structure includes fixed and variable costs that we need to incur so that the solution is provided.

These are very important steps to take during the validation of the idea. Very often the entrepreneur is so in love with his or her idea (or the solution), that it seems difficult to step out of that bubble and put him/herself in the shoes of the end customer. Thus, it is a beneficial exercise to attempt to infer how good the idea is from the client's point of view. If that appreciation is not possible, asking someone to play that role might be necessary. Additionally, it is necessary to align – to the greatest degree possible – all activities that are part of the firm's business process, in an effort to eliminate those that do not create value, reduce those which add little, increase others that are appreciated, and implement new ones that might not be in the original model, but reveal themselves to be important for the success of the business.

How do we develop the 'Value Proposition'?

The most common definition of **value proposition** is "a business or marketing statement used to summarize why a consumer and/or client should buy a product or use a service". Therefore, a value proposition is not a description of the product or service that you agree to deliver to the customer. A value proposition is the ingredient of your business that solves a problem better than competitors. Your value proposition is your unique identifier – which is why it is sometimes called the Unique Selling Proposition. Without it, people don't have a reason to work with you over somebody else. For this reason Value Propositions are sometimes developed along two lines: (1) Employee Value Propositions and (2) Customer Value Propositions (CVP). Some of the differences can be summarized as:

- CVPs describe a solution to a customer's problem. EVPs describe a reward for an employee's talents.
- CVPs explain why someone should buy from you. EVPs explain why someone should work with you.
- CVPs are about you serving the customer. EVPs are about you and the employee serving each other.

What is 'Value Innovation' in the framework of Value Proposition?

Business differentiation might require innovation either in the product/service or in the process of delivering value. A very effective way to develop the Customer Value Proposition is through value innovation, because it leads to a simultaneous pursuit of differentiation and low cost, creating a leap in value for both buyers and the company. Value innovation development can be described as follows:

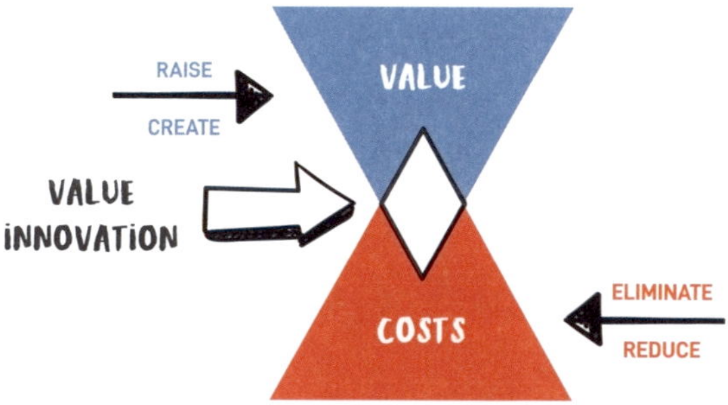

Value Innovation is the simultaneous pursuit of differentiation and low cost, creating a leap in value for both buyers and the company.

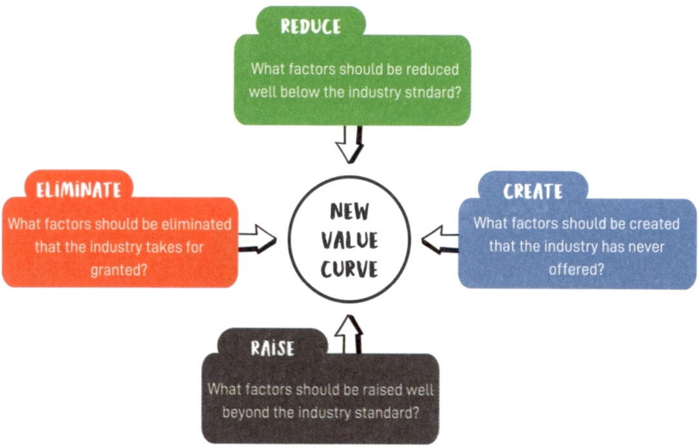

Adapted from: W. Chan Kim and Renée Mauborgne, in the book "Blue Ocean Strategy".

What is cascade analysis for the evaluation of business ideas?

Once business development is starting to be consolidated it is time to do a validation test, which can be repeated later if the result is not positive the first time around. The validation test will include what we call a 'cascade analysis' for the validation of the business idea. This analysis includes a set of questions with a logical sequence:

1. Is there a clear Market based opportunity for the product or service?
YES — If not, STOP!

2. Is there a Team able to bring the product or service to the Market?
YES — If not, STOP!

3. Is there an Economic added value in the process?
YES — If not, STOP!

KEY IDEAS AND REFERENCES FOR MORE INFORMATION

- the business validation must start with the market and also include all of the implementation framework (as the PESTEL analysis)
- it is essential to develop a business simulation and test – it can be somewhat virtual or can even involve prototyping

[1] Williamson, D., Cooke, P., Wyn Jenkins, W. & Moreton, K.M. (2003). Strategic Management and Business Analysis, Elsevier.
[2] Collins, R. (2010). A Graphical Method for Exploring the Business Environment.
[3] Maurya, A. (2012). Running Lean: Iterate from Plan A to a Plan That Works. ISBN-13: 978-1449305178

10

What is a Business Model? And how to develop one?

How to define a Business Model?

To understand what a business model is, the best way is to consider a concept analysis and recognize that it is *'something to do with business'* and it is *'something to do with models'*:

Business: is the activity of buying and selling goods and services – either within a particular company that does this, or work that you do, to earn money.	**Model:** is a representation of something, either as a physical object that is usually smaller than the real object, or as a simple description of the object.

A business is an 'exchange' of products or services where 'value' is generated for all parties involved. A model is a set of procedures that provides a means to transform variable options into specific responses, according to a set of rules. By combining the two we get a basic understanding that a business model is *a representation of how an organization or individual buys and sells goods and services and earns money*. A slightly more elegant definition of a business model might be, "*the process by which an organization creates, delivers, and captures value*", *in economic, social, cultural or other contexts*. When we can establish a process to create, deliver and capture value from a specific set of resources and market flow we have a business model. The process of business model construction is part of the business strategy.

Why it is important to have a business model?

Each business idea will have several possible business models. A business model provides a consistent, repeatable and reliable process to generate economic value. Having a reference model means that we can have global procedures and we can align the market options within the team and the clients, and even define our positioning relating to competitors. Having a model provides guidance for the team and reference for clients and therefore it should communicated to the market, so that stakeholders know what to expect and what to comply with.

How to develop a business model and what are the best practices to start?

There are three best practice methods that can be followed for the development of a specific business model: (1) Always start by evaluating the 'business models' followed by your competitors. If you are going to emulate other business models and explore your competitors' weaknesses, you must know their business models in detail; (2) The business model must also consider that the process must be aligned with providing a fit with the customers' needs; it requires in-depth knowledge – as far as possible – of the client profile; (3) Some disruptive business models can be studied and evaluated for ideas to incorporate into or inspire your business. In the process of developing a business model, an analysis of what others are doing is good practice; this does not mean copying them, but rather, gaining a better understanding of some of the ingredients for success or failure. A few doses of "out-of-the-box" thinking may also be necessary to come up with disruptive solutions that you have not yet come across.

What are the main parameters that define a business model?

The business model can have several layers of detail, depending on the type of business. A restaurant, a web platform, a consulting company or an agriculture business all require a business model but have different levels of complexity. For the sake of clarity we propose three characteristics that are required from a business model regardless of the field of activity. It is very important to explicitly state these, since they will help to set up the underlying business model.

(1) Type of client	(2) Type of need satisfied	(3) Type of relationship with client
B2B of B2C or B2B2C	Position(s) in the Maslow pyramid	One time, multiple

Is it possible to have more than one business model for the same business?

Yes. It is possible to have different 'business models' for the same business. This means that a business model can in fact be a blend of different possible business models put together. However, if this is the case, the different times – and eventually the different markets or locations – in which the different components of the blended business model would be used, should be identified and made explicit. This allows clients to know exactly what to expect. The worst thing that could happen here would be to have clients confused about the strategy undertaken by the company in the different settings considered. Unfortunately, this scenario is rather common. Knowing the business model is also of capital importance for investors.

What is the difference between Business Model and Business Strategy?

The business model is the means of making the business strategy happen. The business strategy is the means by which it sets out to achieve its desired objectives. It can be described simply as a method of long-term business planning. Typically a business strategy will cover a period of about 3-5 years (sometimes even longer). It is not possible to define a strategy without a clear definition of the objectives. The way the strategy is put into practice falls in the business model and assists in defining the money earning logic. The implementation of the strategy is one of the most challenging issues and will concern workflow and the organization of operations. We will see this layer of the process in a subsequent volume of this collection.

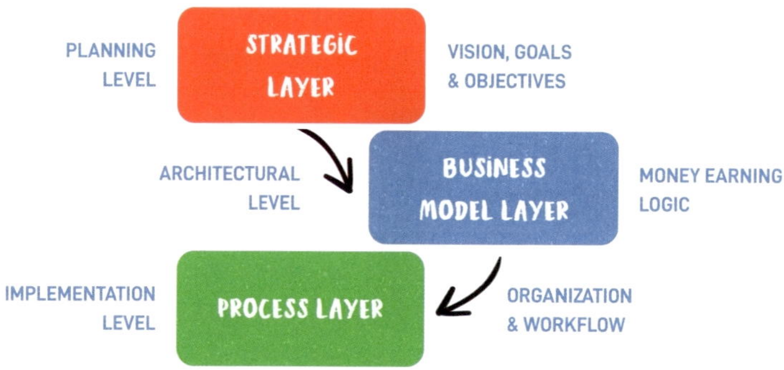

Adapted from [3] Osterwalder, 2004, p. 14

What is the Business Model Canvas?

The Business Model Canvas was proposed in 2008-2010 by Alexander Osterwalder, based on his earlier book: Business Model Ontology. It outlines several prescriptions that form the building blocks for the activities. It enables both new and existing businesses to focus on operational and strategic management and a marketing plan. The Business Model Canvas is a strategic management tool and a template for developing new or documenting existing business models. It is a visual chart with elements describing a firm or product's value proposition, infrastructure, customers, and finances. The Business Model Canvas is not a model itself but a tool to develop models.

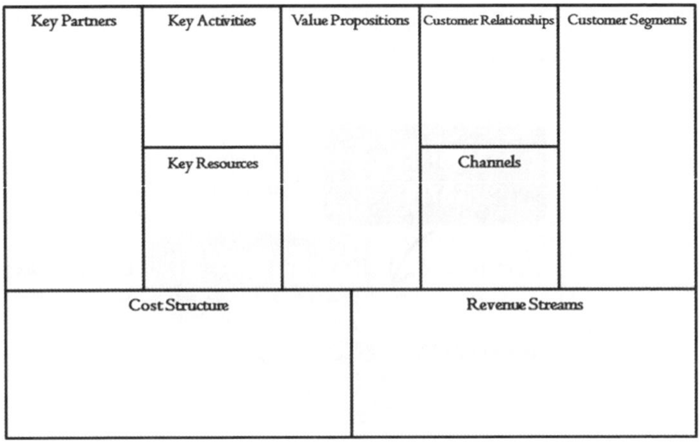

When should the Business Model Canvas be used?

The Canvas is a very good tool for organizing ideas concerning the business development of a specific idea. The process of building it is very important, as it pushes us to think about the building blocks and the way they should be used so that they lead to a revenue logic. The main limitation is that this tool is often used in a simplified way and leads to erroneous conclusions because it is essentially qualitative and generates a sense of easiness. It can be a useful tool for bringing together different information and promoting good discussion and analysis within the core team.

When should the Business Model Canvas not be used?

Some entrepreneurs and consultants believe that just by filling out the squares of a 'business model canvas', they already have a business model. They couldn't be more wrong. As we have said, this framework is essentially qualitative. Therefore it is, most of the time, a declaration of intention, rather than effectively a validation tool. Very often, this framework, suffers from the absence of a quantitative confirmation. This exercise pushes entrepreneurs to anticipate not just the expected cost structure, but – and this is more tricky – the expected profit structure. So this framework helps provide a good list of questions. The real challenge is finding sharp and accurate responses to those questions.

KEY IDEAS AND REFERENCES FOR MORE INFORMATION

- a business model is a process
- the process of business model construction is part of the business strategy

[1] Osterwalder, A, Pigneur, Y. & Smith, A. (2010). Business Model Generation. ISBN: 978-0-470-87641-1 https://strategyzer.com/canvas – https://canvanizer.com/new/business-model-canvas [accessed in 2018 Jan. 20]

[2] Cowan, A. (2018). The 20 Minute Business Plan: Business Model Canvas Made Easy: www.alexandercowan.com/business-model-canvas-templates [accessed in 2018 Jan. 20]

[3] Osterwalder, A. (2004). The Business Model Ontology: A Proposition in a Design Science Approach. Doctoral thesis at the Institut d'Informatique et Organisation. Lausanne, Switzerland, University of Lausanne, HEC.

[4] Kaplan, S. (2012). The Business Model Innovation Factory: How to Stay Relevant When The World is Changing. Hoboken, NJ: Wiley.

11

Which is the best business model for my idea?

What options are there for business models?

There are several possible business models that can be used. However, they all fall, more or less, into one of three categories. This categorization is based on the idea that a business is an exchange. The characteristics in the table headings below reflect the type of possible exchanges there are. Therefore, the three options depend of the type of trade a business establishes with its clients. It is important to point out that very often, different business models can be combined to generate a new one.

Repeated purchase (Σ)	Leveled purchase (±)	Fractionated purchase (%)
– Subscription – Access – Leasing and renting – Franchising	– Low cost – Premium – Hypermarket – Experience	– Free – Commission – Marketplace – Pyramid

How to evaluate the different possible models and rank them?

The evaluation and comparison of possible business models requires the analysis of different options and eventually a simulation for the specific case, according to the idea in question. Some companies combine more than one business model.

Subscription How: **A regular product or service that is provided and that replaces an ad-hoc purchase** Examples: NetFlix, Dollar, Apple music
Free How: **Turn non-paying users into suppliers of something that others will pay for ('if you are not paying for the product, then you are the product')** Examples: Google, Facebook
Premium How: **Free-to-use model giving access to a certain number of features of the value proposition, plus a subscription model for an upgraded version of the value proposition** Examples: Spotify, Linkedin, Dropbox
Access How: **Temporary access to ownership of goods and services through monetization; follows the sharing economy logic** Examples: Zipcar, Peerbuy, AirbnB
On-demand How: **From people with time and no money to people with money and no time** Examples: Uber, Operator, Taskrabbit, Mechanical Turks
Experience How: **Provide a superior experience where payment results from exceeded expectations** Examples: Tesla, Apple
Pyramid How: **Resellers and affiliates that get a commission upon reference of new clients** Examples: Amazon, Microsoft, Dropbox, Bimby, Tupperware, Avon, Yves Rocher

Marketplace – APPROPRIATE FOR LARGE COMPANIES How: **There is a place where the interests of buyers and suppliers are met. And there is a placement fee or commission in exchange of connecting them directly** Examples: eBay, iTunes, Uber AirBnB, OLX
Hypermarket – APPROPRIATE FOR LARGE COMPANIES How: **a market where Brands are sold in scale, to be able to sell at reduced prices** Examples: Amazon, Apple
Ecosystem – APPROPRIATE FOR LARGE COMPANIES How: **Consumer dependency from interlocked and interdependent suite of products and services belonging to one brand (to which they are loyal)** Examples: Apple, Google, Nike, Harley Davidson
Some companies combine more than one business model.

How do we know which are the possible business model options for our idea?

Once we know what a business model is, what types of model exist and which are the most common, we have the task of deciding which models can be used for our business. One of the things that characterizes an entrepreneur is his/her ability to see opportunities where others see nothing. This is because they have normally mastered a particular competence during their lives, which is normally combined with other skills. Their practical sense for using their feelings in selecting business models for latent and existent opportunities is relevant in this process. We understand this is what makes them experts in their field. Becoming an expert in a specific area is therefore of utmost importance. An entrepreneur has a feeling that an opportunity has room to be developed under a certain business model. It is often an educated hunch. Aside from that, they must have mastery of an area where the seed they plant may flourish. Intuition must be accompanied by specialist knowledge in a certain field, since the only way to choose is on the basis of educated information or in-depth knowledge. An entrepreneur who is very familiar with the proposed area of work will sense the possible options.

How to choose the best business model within the different possibilities?

There is no best business model 'for everyone, everything and any time'. A good practice strategy that is used to evaluate the options for the different business models, for a specific opportunity, is to set up a comparison table with a ranking system. The proposed approach is to classify each business model option, according to three performance ratios, called the 3 Es. The ranking provides some criteria for the possible options.

Efficiency	Efficacy	Effectiveness
= Results / Resources	= Results / Objectives	= (+) or (–) Results

For each specific business model it is possible to evaluate or simulate performance, measuring the ratio of expected Results to affected Resources; the ratio of expected Results to the initial Objectives; and the simplest analysis of the results shown. This approach pushes us to use quantitative parameters in the analysis. Normally, the final analysis and decision is based only on the feelings that entrepreneurs and other consultants have about what they expect the outcomes to be. However, a professional analysis cannot be driven by this simplistic approach.

For the implementation of this analytical rationale, we should keep in mind that several factors should be considered:

The nature of the business	The opportunity framework or *momentum*	The team that implements it
Production or services	The triggers or motivations to implement	The background of the business

As we can see, efficacy depends on the nature of the business, the *momentum* in which the business is being considered, as well as the team involved in its implementation.

Why it is important to combine the business model for a specific team and time frame?

Even the best business model may fail if two other factors are absent: the time frame (*momentum*) and the right team. In fact, this is a very important and relevant question and there is an easy answer: the best business model for a specific idea is the one that provides the best results, taking into account the team that is going to implement the business. So, taken in an isolated manner, a business opportunity may mean nothing. Its appropriateness cannot be considered without these two factors. Hence, the response to this question is not easy or immediate; the "best" business model is the one that provides better results for the promoting team, at that moment in time.

Why it is important to combine business models for a specific opportunity?

Among the three most relevant ways of deciding which business model to choose for a certain business opportunity, the deductive-inductive process is often the most appropriate for an entrepreneur. Most of the time, however, entrepreneurs don't gain the necessary expertise before using their intuition. Under these circumstances, they make decisions without having the appropriate background – they are not experts – and in many ways this may lead to failure. We cannot emphasize this point strongly enough: before becoming an entrepreneur, you should become an expert. Making decisions without the relevant expertise is dangerous and may lead to failure. If this is a dangerous situation for anyone, it is even more dangerous for entrepreneurs, who normally have the impression they are more skilled at making decisions and taking risks than others. This means that warning signals may be more easily ignored by entrepreneurs than by other people.

A deductive process	An inductive process	A deductive-inductive process
Follows a logical process: if A=B, then A+C=B+C This process compares items with one another	Feelings-based process Results from the study if several similar situations Based on experience and intuition	A dual combination of the two earlier processes
A niche approach	The most common process	The best approach

We have now learned that it is of the utmost importance to be – or to become – a specialist in your field of work. To know whether the responses obtained for the above criteria are good enough to allow you to move forward, you need to be a specialist in your field. We believe in educated information/knowledge as the basis for decision making. However, many people have used this kind of approach without having become specialists beforehand. We do not endorse this approach. Market information is critical in this process, both for the validation of a business idea, as well as for the development of any business.

KEY IDEAS AND REFERENCES FOR MORE INFORMATION

- simulation is a best practice way of evaluating and ranking a possible business case model
- the process of selection requires a deductive-inductive approach where time and the team play critical roles.

[1] A comprehensive list of Business Models to accelerate you and your business. (2016). International Six Sigma Institute™ www.sixsigma-institute.org/blog/A-Comprehensive-List-of-Business-Models-To-Accelerate-You-and-Your-Business [accessed in 2018 Jan. 20]

[2] Caudron, J. & and Van Peteghem, D. (2017). Digital transformation in business – www.digitaltransformationbook.com [accessed in 2018 Jan. 20]

12

How to evaluate the Market?

What is the concept of 'the Market'?

The Market is an actual or nominal place where forces of demand and supply operate, and where buyers and sellers interact (directly or through intermediaries) to trade goods, services, contracts or instruments, for money or barter. Markets include mechanisms or means for (1) determining the price of the traded item, (2) communicating the price information, (3) facilitating deals and transactions, and (4) effecting distribution. The market for a particular item is made up of existing and potential customers who need it and have the ability and willingness to pay for it. Markets can exist physically or not.

How to calculate the size of the market?

This is a very important question that normally people have great difficulty in answering. When evaluating market size there are three things to consider: (1) the market size in quantity = number of units sold; (2) the market value in monetary units or currency = quantity multiplied by the unitary price; (3) market growth over time, usually expressed in a % growth per year. One possible way to evaluate the size of the market is to determine the number of clients and the value that each client is willing to pay for the product or service in different time frames. Another way is to evaluate the sales value of the main players for our specific segment over time. The two ways should result in similar values.

What is the market that our product/service should target?

To answer this question, the following key concepts are relevant. For the sake of clarity we will use the analysis of the market of a university canteen as an example:

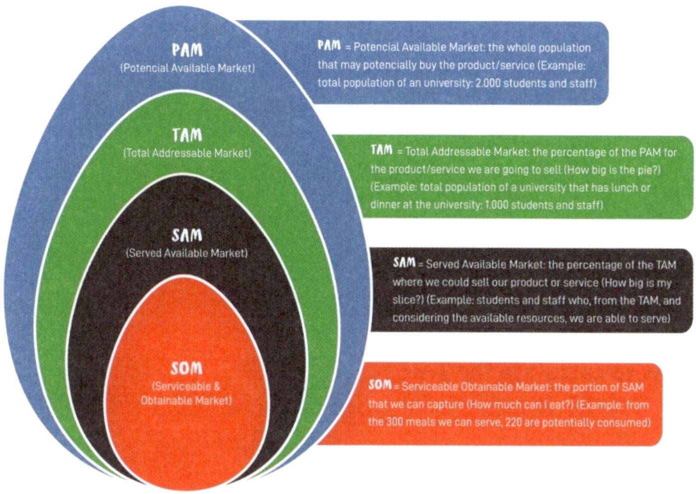

PAM = Potential Available Market: the whole population that may potentially buy the product/service (Example: total population of an university: 2000 students and staff)

TAM = Total Addressable Market: the percentage of the PAM for the product /service we are going to sell (> How big is the pie?) (Example: total population of a university that has lunch or dinner at the university: 1000 students and staff)

SAM = Served Available Market: the percentage of the TAM where we could sell our product or service (> how big is my slice?) (Example: students and staff who, from the TAM, and considering the available resources, we are able to serve)

SOM = Serviceable Obtainable Market: the portion of SAM that we can capture (> how much can I eat?) (Example: from the 300 meals we can serve, 220 are potentially consumed)

TM = Target Market: this is the amount of money we can make from SOM (Example: if 220 people turn up and each spends an average of 4 euros, we can make 880 euros).

What is the meaning of Available, Addressable and Obtainable?

(1) Available: represents an upper limit of market opportunity – what you could aspire to pursue long-term if you had the breadth and depth of offerings and market coverage.

(2) Addressable: the potential of the market for you and your competitors. Venture Capitalist care a lot about this as it represents the extent of the particular arena in which you compete.

(3) Obtainable: represents what is realistically within your reach, given factors such as sales coverage, product attributes, competitive entrenchment, and resource limitations.

How to calculate the TAM?

There are three distinct ways to calculate TAM:

1) Top-down, using industry research and reports or other available documents where that data may be informed. This makes a strong case for the regular reading of documents concerning the business field in which we wish to become experts.
2) Bottom-up, using data from early selling efforts or available resources/capacity. It may take the form of "Here's how we price and how many units of that price we can sell." This is a much better option than the first, because it involves tangible, relatable data on current pricing/usage of the product. Extrapolation may be used. Nevertheless, the extrapolation procedure is conducted on the basis of solid numbers.
3) Value theory, using conjecture about buyers' willingness to pay. This is a more risky option that should be kept for cases in which the previous two options cannot be used. It takes the form of "Here's how much value we can create, and why we'll be able to capture it." The

value-theory TAM relies on an estimate of the value provided to a set of users by the product, as well as a guess at how much of that value creation can be captured through pricing. It is therefore more appropriate for new products.

How to calculate the SOM?

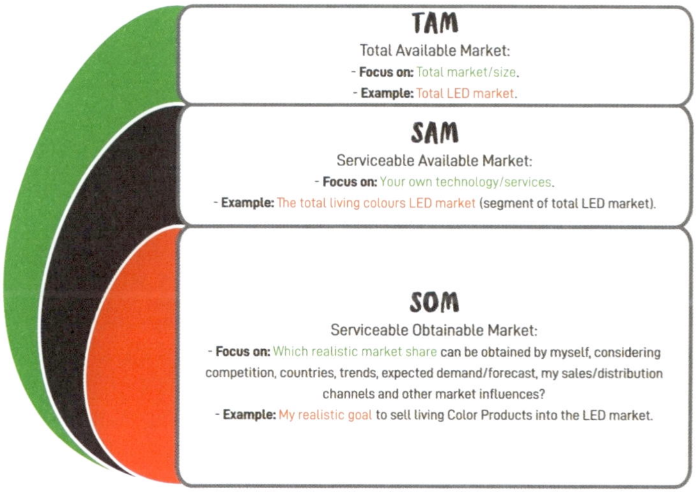

The Serviceable and Obtainable Market (SOM) is critical market information because it combines the two most important variables required to evaluate the potential deployment of the business:

1) average price the clients are willing to pay;
2) average number of potential clients

KEY IDEAS AND REFERENCES FOR MORE INFORMATION

- without strong evidences (market research based) that there is a market related opportunity there are high chances of failure
- market research must be done by or with the entrepreneurs otherwise there is a strong possibility that it is not focused on the critical issues

[1] Zafar, N. (2010). Market Research on a Shoestring. ISBN-13: 978-0982342046
[2] Weinberg, G. (2015). Traction: How Any Startup Can Achieve Explosive Customer Growth

13

How to differentiate from competitors?

Why is it necessary to guarantee a distinctive character to our business?

Distinction is relevant in different stages of a business. This involves distinction from competitors' products, as well as from the firm's other products. To be relevant it is necessary that the manner in which we are different is perceived by clients in the intended way. This means that we need to carefully think about the way we want them to see us, and try to imprint that in their minds. Being different from what already exists is important, but more than that, it is important that our clients effectively *perceive* us as different. And thinking carefully about this also means bearing in mind what resources we have at our disposal, what our strengths are, but also our weaknesses. In many business we see entrepreneurs who believe firmly that they are different because of what they do. However, they seem to be unable to read clients' understanding of the new business and therefore they operate on skewed premises.

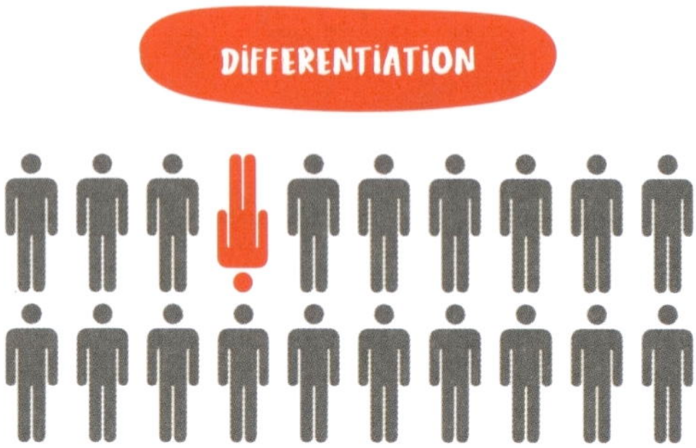

DRIVERS OF DIFFERENTIATION

UNIQUE PRODUCTS FEATURES
UNIQUE PRODUCT PERFORMANCE
EXCEPTIONAL SERVICES
NEW TECHNOLOGIES
QUALITY INPUTS
EXCEPTIONAL SKILL OR EXPERIENCE
DETAILED INFORMATION

Adapted from www.openlearningworld.com accessed in 2018 Jan. 20

What happens if you do not care in detail about your differentiation?

If a business does not voluntarily decide in which way it wants to stand out from the rest, it risks not being sufficiently different, or being differentiated in the wrong way. When clients do not understand our positioning in the way we intend, they may not appreciate the difference we wanted them to perceive. If we do not present a clear and focused difference, the market will tend to pulverize our business's image, and we run a real risk of being indistinguishable. Due to competitive forces in the market, it is difficult to maintain differentiation indefinitely, so regular renovation is advisable. If you do not actively decide and plan for this, the market will do it for you – but not usually in the direction you would like.

What is the impact of the difference chosen?

When you have chosen a difference on which to build up the business, it is important to consider the pros and cons of that option. In fact, there are positive and negative impacts of this decision. Thus, a tradeoff analysis must be conducted. For instance, if a company chooses to produce vegan shoes, it makes a difference and is likely to be chosen by clients who value that characteristic. However, by having made that choice, the company excludes itself from working with other materials, such as, for instance, leather, which can be good for the production of sneakers. This means that all the pros and cons of each one of the options should be accessed carefully, before deciding.

Positives	Negatives
One positive of a successful differentiation strategy is that the organization may charge a premium for its product or service. The company does so with confidence because it has a reputation of being good at this. The company can readily pass along higher supplier costs to its customers because of the lack of substitute products on the market. Having a loyal customer basis helps stabilize the company's revenue and lessens the impact of market downturns because of customer loyalty through both good times and bad.	A company that succeeds in implementing a differentiation strategy must worry about competitors copying and being attracted by its success. In addition, implementing a differentiation strategy is costly and it may take years before a company achieves a strong brand image and reputation that allows it to be different. During that time, the company faces the risk of changing consumer preferences. In such a case, the company may not have sufficient customer demand to offset its higher costs, which may lead to a loss.

Where can differentiation be noted?

Regardless of the way in which being different is built, it is important that it is part of the business's DNA. This means that the difference chosen should be omnipresent in the company strategy and it should be reflected in the way the business is conducted. Therefore, it is important that all elements somehow connected to the company follow this philosophy in each and every way they act. Differentiation is usually led by some source of innovation and therefore it is very important to know how to promote innovation in the business development process. Differentiation should be within the corporate culture, corresponding to the following option:

The 1st choice for clients	The 1st choice for employees	The 1st choice for investors
Our offer of products or services is preferred over all others within its chosen markets	Our business is the preferred place to work within its geographical location(s).	Our business outperforms its competitors by delivering higher value to shareholders

In which way can a business distinguish itself?

There are many ways to build up a distinguishable approach in a business, either related to products or services. Differentiation can be in any and all levels of the business, from the products or services to the business model. All differentiation options fall into one or two of three approaches: (1) innovation, (2) cost driven and (3) customer intimacy. However, they cannot be chosen simultaneously, with the same weight given to each. This means that a more innovative approach can be followed with some level of customer intimacy, but not with the same importance as a cost-driven approach, for instance.

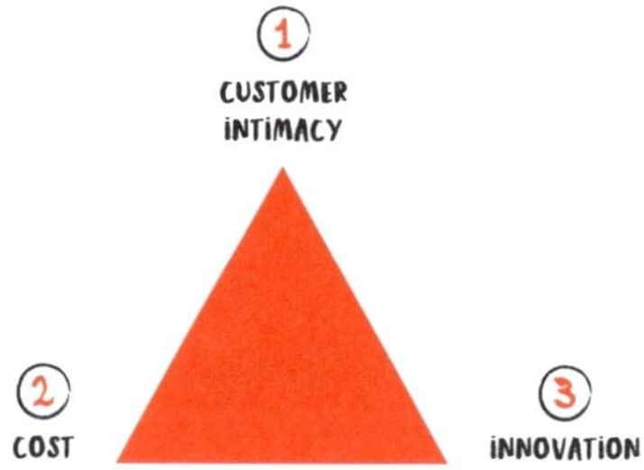

- Customer intimacy: even though this is possible to obtain better in a B2B scenario, it is also possible to work in a B2C context; it refers to the trust the client places in the value proposition offered which leads him/her to go beyond preference, it takes the shape of investment in the development of trusting relationships
- Cost-driven: it refers to building up a value proposition that has the cost as the main factor: it can be low, high or somewhere in between, depending on how the business wants its difference to be understood
- Innovation: it refers to the creation of new approaches to the product (or its process of production) perceived by the clients as such

KEY IDEAS AND REFERENCES FOR MORE INFORMATION

- innovation is the preferred form of differentiation for all business
- differentiation is critical for a competitive position in the market and relevant exploitation of the 'value proposition'

[1] Trout, J. & Rivkin, S. (2001). Differentiate or Die: Survival in Our Era of Killer Competition. New Jersey: Wiley

[2] Moon, Y. (2011). Different: Escaping the Competitive Herd. New York, NY

14

What are the motivations and processes for innovation?

What is Business Innovation?

Innovation generally refers to changing processes or creating more effective processes, products and ideas. For businesses, this could mean implementing new ideas, creating dynamic products or improving their existing services. Innovation can increase the likelihood of your business succeeding. Business innovation is therefore an organization's process for introducing new ideas, workflows, methodologies, services or products.

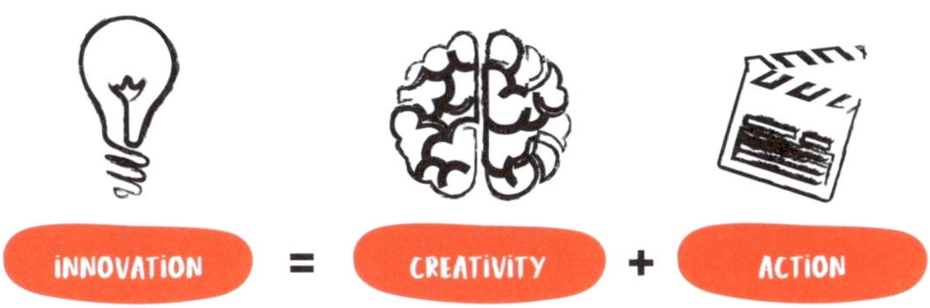

What are the types of innovation that are relevant for business development?

There are three ascending levels of innovation that is possible to follow. The level you choose will dictate the simplicity or complexity of the journey you will undertake. Unfortunately, far too many companies expect to achieve the highest levels of innovation while only providing the strategy, tools, and support for lower-level success, at best. The three levels are:

1. Incremental Innovation. This consists of small, yet meaningful improvements in your products, services, and other ways in which you do business. These tend to be the "new and improved" innovations we are all bombarded with every day: new flavors, shifts to better or all-natural ingredients, packaging improvements, faster/slower functioning, just-in-time supply chain enhancements, bigger/smaller sizing, cost reductions, heavier/lighter weight. We see them every day and they help extend product, service, and business life cycles and improve profitability. They can be easily visualized and quickly communicated and give you something new with which to grab consumer attention in an increasingly noisy marketplace.
2. Breakthrough Innovation. This is a meaningful change in the way you do business that gives consumers something demonstrably new (beyond "new and improved"). Breakthrough innovation produces a substantial competitive edge for a while, although the length of time anyone can maintain such an advantage is growing increasingly shorter.
3. Transformational Innovation. This is usually (but not always) the introduction of a technology that creates a new industry and transforms the way we live and work. This kind of innovation often eliminates existing industries or, at a minimum, totally transforms them. For this reason, transformational innovations tend to be championed by those who aren't wedded to an existing infrastructure. Transformational innovation is exceedingly rare. Think about it: how many truly new-to-the-world ideas happen in a year? In a lifetime? Not many!

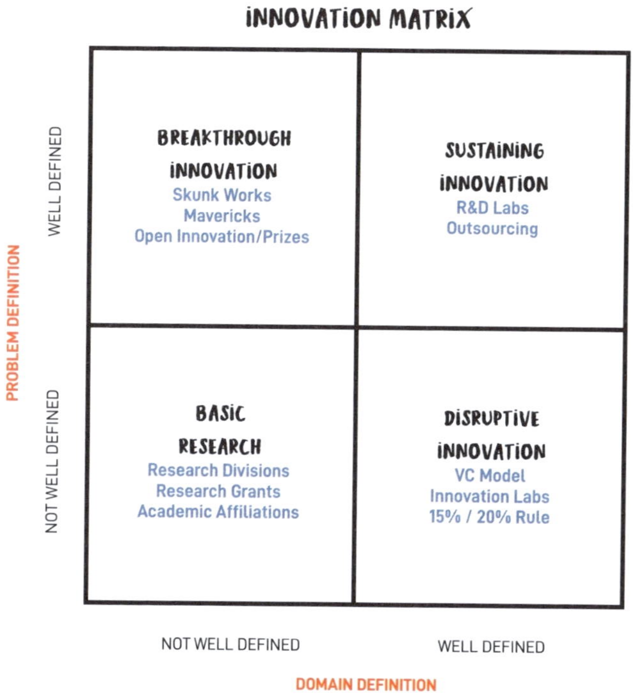

adapted from mapping Innovation [3]

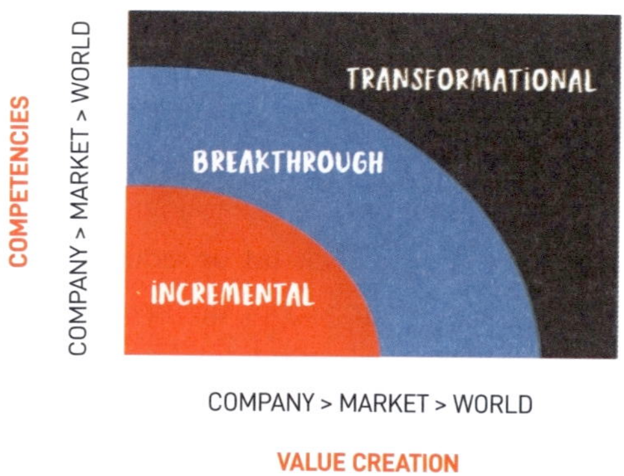

adapted from creative realities [4]

What is the difference between Innovation and Invention?

Many people do not understand the difference between innovation and invention. In a business, the critical factor is not invention, but innovation. Invention refers to the creation of a completely new product, device or production process. Conversely, innovation is an act of making changes to the existing product or process, by introducing new ways or ideas. Tom Grasty, for PBS Idea Lab (March 29, 2012), elegantly summarized: "If invention is a pebble tossed in the pond, innovation is the rippling effect that the pebble causes. Someone has to toss the pebble and that is the inventor. Someone has to recognize the ripple will eventually become a wave and that is the innovator or entrepreneur. Entrepreneurs do not stop at the water's edge. They watch the ripples and spot the next big wave before it happens. And it's the act of anticipating and riding that 'next big wave' that drives the innovative nature in every entrepreneur."

What are the drivers or parameters of our business where we can innovate?

We may innovate in several ways. The following set of questions should be considered as a check-list or sequence where innovation is possible and has impact in the business. The answers will lead to relevant contributions for business development because will connect innovation, differentiation and purpose. The ultimate purpose is always business value.

What is the need we address?	→ What is our selling / value proposition?
Who has the need that we are addressing (clients)?	→ Market Analysis ← Market Research
Why are we addressing that need?	→ What is our differentiation?
What is our positioning towards competitors?	→ What is our competitive advantage?
What is our positioning towards clients?	→ How do we define prices and make proposals?

These questions drive decisions concerning innovation. If we address the above questions we are more likely to be successful in innovating our business. Very often, when business fail, we will see that it is because the product or service the company created didn't successfully address these questions.

What is the role of innovation in business development?

Innovation should always be part of the business development process because it is a key differentiation factor. Innovation is very important in business because the other two ways to be competitive are in price and customer intimacy and neither of these is sustainable over time, or easy to achieve (even in the short run). That is why many entrepreneurs bet on being innovative. However, it will only pay off, if and when it is put into practice. Otherwise, it won't be more than just an idea. Innovation will only produce results if it can be applied. Hence, a market analysis must be conducted first, so that we are able to understand whether there is room for innovation, and what type of innovation this should be.

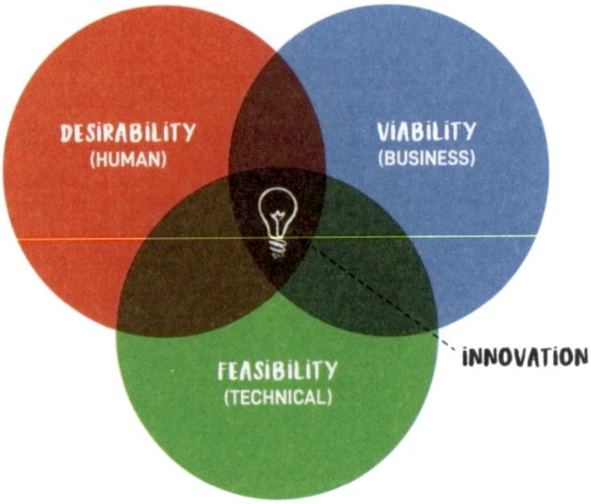

and

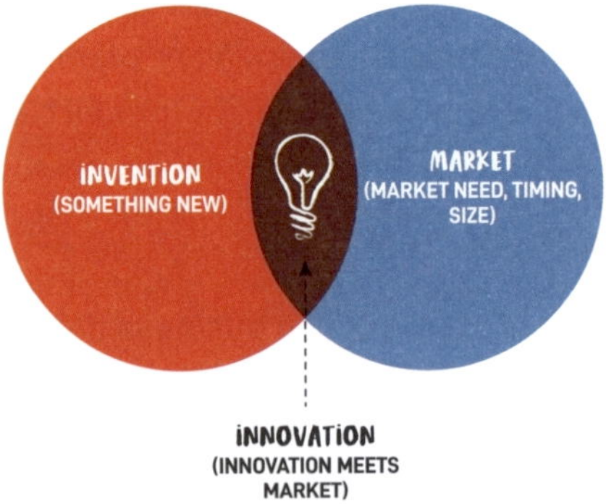

KEY IDEAS AND REFERENCES FOR MORE INFORMATION

- a solution for a problem is an innovation if it get to the implementation stage; otherwise it is just a inventive idea or a concept
- there are a wide range of possible innovation strategies or processes that also lead to a variety of results with different levels of impact

[1] Dealing with Darwin: How Great Companies Innovate at Every Phase of Their Evolution.

[2] de Jong, M., Marston, N. & Roth, E. (2015) The eight essentials of innovation.

[3] Satell, G. (2017). Mapping Innovation: A Playbook for Navigating a Disruptive Age.

[4] Terwilliger, J. (2015). The Three Levels of Innovation. Posted on September 30, 2015 – www.creativerealities.com [accessed in 2018 Jan. 20]

15

How to innovate in the process of business development?

How can the innovation process be planned and managed?

The purpose of innovation is 'simply' to create business value ('simply', because it's easier said than done!), but the value itself can take many different forms. The method of creating innovation is to discover, create, and develop ideas, to refine them into useful forms, and to use them to earn profits, increase efficiency, and/or reduce costs. Innovation management describes the decisions, activities, and practices that move an idea to realization for the purpose of generating business value. It is managing the investment in creating new opportunities for generating customer value that are needed to sustain and grow the business or company. Hence, we can say that the process can and should be carefully planned and managed. One of the most useful tools for this is the innovation master plan.

What is the Innovation Master Plan?

A powerful way to think about this, and to devise an Innovation Master Plan is through five simple questions – the five simplest imaginable: Why? What? How? Who? Where?

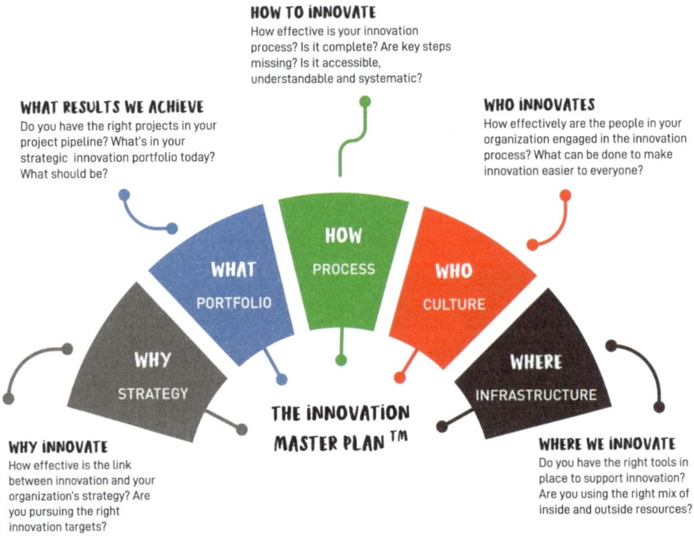

Adapted from Agile Innovation Master Plan Framework in www.innovationlabs.com accessed on Jan 20, 2018.

What are the European Innovation Management Standards?

The European Innovation Management Standards can be a source of inspiration to develop and validate the conclusions from the innovation master plan, providing a set of possible ways to structure the innovation before market testing. The European Innovation Management Standard CEN/TS 16555 has been in place since 2008, and as such it incorporates a lot of the elements that are believed to constitute current best practices on innovation management. It is worth studying them. The Standard consists of seven documents that can be followed to organize the Innovation Master Plan:

Innovation management system (16555-1:2013)
Strategic intelligence management (16555-2:2014)
Innovation thinking (16555-3:2014)
Intellectual property management (16555-4:2014)
Collaboration management (16555-5:2014)
Creativity management (16555-6:2014)
Innovation management assessment (16555-7,2015)

What are the different ways to promote and implement innovations?

There are more than 500 different innovation management systems. This has so much relevance for firms currently, that IT-based solutions alone are not enough to solve all firms' challenges. As a matter of fact, part of the challenge concerning innovation management is collecting and evaluating ideas in the initial phases. IT solutions help benchmark what has been done, but they do not assist in applying the benchmarks to the specific need in question. When companies are evaluated about innovation management, very often the conversation revolves around having an innovation management system, but in a very narrow sense. The sentence, "We need a system", more often than not implies a wish for an IT-based system to handle idea management. There are plenty of such systems around, and they are getting fancier every day. However, we believe that just as important as collecting information about innovations is actually applying it.

It could be said that there are basically two ways of promoting the innovation: (1) brainstorming everyone in the firm, so that people are aware of the importance of their ideas for innovation; and (2) creating task forces for the implementation of the ideas generated.

What are the possible ways to apply innovation?

There are four main types or directions of innovations that represent the foundation of new companies. Achievements related to these can be considered within the firm's innovation master plan.

We pursue breakthroughs to attain major competitive advantage. Breakthroughs are distinguished from incremental innovations, as those are "just" minor improvements to existing business structures, processes, and products.
We invest in incremental innovation to maintain or improve market share. New venture innovations extend existing companies into new markets.
We create new ventures to expand into new markets for long-term benefit, creating new and better customer experiences.
We create new business models to transform the structure of a market; New business models are new ways of making money.

How to design and implement the innovation master plan

The best practice strategy to develop, prepare and manage innovation portfolios is to adopt the following 5 steps:

1. Model the Key Strategic Factors in the business sector
2. Define the characteristics or criteria to be considered for the innovation
3. Define the weighting of the characteristics and score them in terms of attractiveness.
4. Assess the Risk-Reward associated with the each item, within the business sector, and define the ideal Innovation Portfolio.
5. Assess proposed new projects using a Risk-Reward assessment tool, concerning the proposed projects.

KEY IDEAS AND REFERENCES FOR MORE INFORMATION

- The 'Innovation Masterplan" is a very useful tool to manage innovation in a startup as supports the innovation driver across the organization
- It is as important to promote innovation as a differentiation factor, as it is to manage develop a continuous innovation process in the organization

[1] Ries, E. (2017). The Startup Way: How Entrepreneurial Management Transforms Culture and Drives Growth.
[2] Maital, S. & Seshadri, D. (2013). Innovation Management: Strategies, Concepts and Tools for Growth and Profit.

16

What is a Business Case? How does it compare with a Business Plan?

What is a Business Case?

A business case is an executive document that describes, in a condensed number of pages, a specific business. It covers the business idea, the business model, the market it addresses, the implementation of the 'go to market' approach, the organization of the team, and the profit and loss, including the necessary investment and the performance of the business.

What is a Business Plan?

The business plan is a descriptive document that presents, over the necessary number of pages (usually in the range of 80-160), all the details of a specific business and its implementation. More than simply a plan, this document also sets out how the business is supposed to be developed. It must include specific chapters such as the Market study, the Team and their profile, the Marketing plan and a detailed financial plan with a comprehensive investment analysis.

What are the main differences between a Business Case and a Business Plan?

Business Case	Business Plan
– It is the preferred tool for small business development	– Usually used and required for larger business
– Large businesses are often divided in several smaller ones	– Sometimes clusters of small businesses require plans
– The focus is the business development	– The focus is the business presentation
– Typically an internal document for the team	– Typically a document for investors or stakeholders
– A 2 or 3 page document with annexes	– An 80+ page document, with annexes
– Easy and fast to update	– Difficult and time-consuming to update
– Involves the entire team in all the parts of the document	– Division of labour can occur among different authors
– The use of infographics and tables is common	– Descriptive explanations are usually preferred
– The whole team must know the document in detail	– It is difficult for all team members to know about all parts of the plan

When is the Business Plan required?

A business plan is necessary when it is required by the person in charge of the decision to implement the idea. Typically banks, investors or providers of subsidies often require a business plan. The target is a prospect or a client, and if a business plan is required, there is no doubt about the need to do it. However, for most of team members and for most of the activities involved, a business case is sufficient.

When is the Business Plan more relevant than a Business Case?

The preference for a business plan over a business case usually arises because the plan provides more information of a quantitative nature, which generates a sense of confidence. With a business plan it is possible to have many pages of relevant information such as the CV of the key team members, market and detailed financial information, etc. Even though this may be considered self due diligence (and therefore possibly biased), it promotes trust.

Why is a Business Case sometimes preferred?

There are three mains reasons to prefer a business case to a business plan:

Faster to read	Easier to change or adapt	More executive
As a rule of thumb, one page of double-spaced, 12-point text will take slightly less than two minutes to read at a reasonable pace. A Business Case is typically a 2-page document to read in less than 5 minutes. The document will generate a 'like' or 'don't like' response, avoiding grey areas.	To change a document with two or three pages is much easier than to change one of 60 to 80 pages. The most difficult part is changing the relationships and implications. The Business Plan is a document that may take up to 60 minutes to read.	The requirement to have a short document with tables and info graphics will also be structured using bullet points. This approach creates a more executive document targeting the implementation rather than the presentation.

How to transform a Business Case into a Business Plan?

The transformation of a business case into a business plan is a simple process of expansion. What is usually included as an annex to the business case is made part of the body of the document. The items in the business plan must be those requested by the specific application. As an example, many venture capital companies or banks have specific templates with their preferred summary and table of contents.

What makes a good Business Case?

The 'quality' of a business case depends largely on the team that develops it! But the most important factor to consider is whether its mission is fit for purpose. A good business case for one context might not be the best for another. It is of critical importance to adapt or adjust the document according to the objectives and purpose. The business case must be also aligned with any pitch or presentation that is required. There are several best practices when it comes to developing and writing a business case that provide much better – i.e. more effective – documents: (1) the use of infographics; (2) the compact nature of the document – typically 2 or 3 pages; (3) lean, concise writing with short and simple sentences – typically the length of a Tweet; (4) the use of support documents as appendices for complimentary information; (5) credibility of the sources that might be referred to.

KEY IDEAS AND REFERENCES FOR MORE INFORMATION

- the 'business case' as a document to guide business development is increasingly the preferred option because of flexibility
- debating which is better – a business case or a business plan – is a nonsense as each has a different focus and usefulness

[1] Van Der Pijl, P. & Lokitz, J. (2016). Design a Better Business: New Tools, Skills, and Mindset for Strategy and Innovation

[2] Kenny, G. (2016). Strategic Plans Are Less Important than Strategic Planning. Harvard Business Review, June 21

17

How is a Business Case structured?

How relevant is it to follow a specific structure, and why?

A reference structure provides several advantages.

(1) It guarantees that all the critical items are covered;
(2) provides an easier understanding;
(3) facilitates a comparative process for benchmarking.

The structure is very important because it impacts the content and therefore the 'message'. The size of each set of items is a reference and not a strict requirement so that the business case can be a compact and executive document that describes a specific business.

1. THE BUSINESS IDEA (1 or 2 page)
What is the *product and/or service idea* definition (= offer) and related *'value proposition'* (1)? In 2 Tweets max.
What is the definition of the *Need* that is satisfied by the product and/or service? In 2 Tweets max.
What is the opportunity framework (=why) motivations and expectation for the development of the business idea?
What is the business? How will the product and/or service idea turn into a *business* (= transaction with added value)?
What is the background for the idea development? *Why?*
What is the *business model* to be followed? (2)
> Business concept validation based on the capacity to address a **specific need**
2. THE MARKET (1 or 2 page)
Who are the *competitors*? (establish a reference to the benchmarks) follow the definition (3)
Who are the *clients*? (Typically, the same as the clients of the competitors).
Define the *qualitative client profiling* so that it is possible to estimate the number of clients for each profile
Define the *quantitative client profile*: who / how many, where, and how much are they willing to pay for the offer?
Develop Market *segmentation growth* based on the integration of Client Profiling information
Define the *differentiation* factor and provide a statement of risk analysis referring to the market-related 'barriers to entry'
> Market validation through **competitor analysis** and customer **profiling**

Why algorithm-based heuristics?

The algorithm approach provides a logical and coherent path that can be followed for most businesses. The majority of questions that arise are common to many business frameworks, as well as the related possible answers. Developing problem-solving, learning, or discoveries that employ practical methods, is not guaranteed to be optimal or perfect, but may be sufficient for immediate goals. It is also important to consolidate the learning process in a shorter time.

Why is important to have reference definitions?

Definitions are essential to guarantee that different people, with different views and backgrounds, can evaluate a document and interpret each relevant concept in the same way. Without definitions to refer to, it is not possible to know whether the answers to the questions follow the objectives of the questions. Reference definitions for business are like the standards for industry.

3. THE OPERATION (1 or 2 page)
Who are the *team* members and what is the necessary expertise they have to develop the business (team profile)? What are the *additional functional competences* required for a complete team? And why? What will the *'production'* plan for *product and/or service* development and delivery look like? Define access to clients and related *barriers* that might exist and how these will be overcome Define *partnerships* and relationships with suppliers, distributors and establish the *'business value chain'* (5) How will the *'go to market'* plan and related communication and marketing strategy (use the Ps approach) (4) look? > Operation validation through the information about **team** resources for the 'go to market'
4. THE PROFIT AND LOSS (1 or 2 page)
What is the *prospective production* plan in the first 6 semesters? What are the prospective *investment* costs (CAPEX) in the same period? What are the expected *operation* costs (OPEX) What are the *prospective sales* or turnover in the first 6 semesters? What are the *results* and eventually the *key performance ratios* (IRR, ROI, PayBack time, other)? What is the *risk analysis* that can be traced and the impact of different scenarios? > Validation through the reasonability of prospective quantitative **performance ratios**
* **Each question requires a summarizing paragraph (max. 2 tweets) or a line in a table or a part in a small infographic – 1 tweet = 140 characters = understood as a possible criteria for the ideal number of characters to define a message...** ** Key definitions: (1) **value proposition** = "a business or marketing statement used to summarize why a consumer and/or client should buy a product or use a service"; (2) **business model** = how an organization creates, delivers, and captures value; (3) **competitors** = "the organizations that provide an answer to the same need"; (4) **the Ps approach** = "the Marketing plan according to the P keywords"; (5) **business value chain** = "set of steps from production, distribution, retail to the Consumer".

KEY IDEAS AND REFERENCES FOR MORE INFORMATION

- the structure of a business case must be adapted for each purpose – there is no universal structure – just a best practice based proposal
- the 'business case' must be a compact document, the concepts and ideas for the different items must be very clear and according to definitions

[1] Dib, A. (2016). The 1-Page Marketing Plan: Get New Customers, Make More Money, And Stand Out From The Crowd.

[2] Schmidt, M.J. (2009). Business Case Essentials: A Guide to Structure and Content. Boston: Solution Matrix ltd, USA

18

How to present a Business Case?

What kinds of options do we have for preparing a business presentation?

In 'business development jargon', a 'business presentation' is commonly referred to as a 'business pitch'. It is usually a presentation designed for investors or stakeholders. There are two options that can be considered when deciding to develop a 'pitch', and the two can be used in combination:

Use a template	Create a new approach from scratch
(+) Fast, simple, easy to develop	Original, customized
(–) Less effective because can generate less impact	Time-consuming, requires more design skills

What is the 'pitch deck' or 'pitch master'?

Employing best practices when developing presentations requires the production of a pitch deck. This is a master document with a wide range of pitch slides that can be tailored to suit different specific pitch versions according to the objectives and audience. The core of the pitch is usually: (1) Slogan; (2) Problem; (3) Solution; (4) Value; (5) Market and revenue model; (6) Team; (7) Execution; (8), Repeat the Slogan and add the Call to Action. There are typically two or three slides per topic. These are the starting topics for building the pitch master. The most common software tools are MS Powerpoint, Adobe PDF and Prezi.

What are the different types of pitch?

There is a general consensus in the 'business development' community that there are three types of investor pitch that should be considered and followed according to the situation:

Elevator pitch	This is typically a one minute pitch that will tell someone what your product or service is Within a **1 minute** elevator ride. An elevator pitch must be concise (never more than 1 minute) and meet three key characteristics: (1) clear (no jargon) (2) compelling (induces a teaser effect), and (3) irrefutable (statements you make are hard to deny).
Short form pitch	This is typically where you will speak more about your company. It is typically **5-10 minutes** long and should include some basics about your company, such as (1) the problem you are solving (2) your solution (3) your team members (4) the market you are in (5) the competition (6) some financial highlights, goals you want to reach (7) and information about your founding team and investors.
Long form pitch	The long form pitch is a formal pitch that tells investors everything they need to know about your company to invest in it. For the long form pitch, it is considered a best practice to use Guy Kawasaki's 30/20/10 rule (proposed in 2006 in https://guykawasaki.com/the_102030_rule/) that states: (1) font size should be no smaller than 30 points (2) the pitch should be no longer than **20 minutes**, and (3) should use no more than 10 slides (which is to say, keep it short – up to 20 slides is okay but no more) You want to pitch your venture in a way that the investors will get your point and want to learn more.

What makes a great pitch ?

The highest impact factor for a pitch is its 'fit to purpose'. That means the pitch is appropriate for the audience and combines excellent content with an excellent presentation. To do that, it is necessary to produce many versions and simulate the presentation, rehearsing as many times as necessary. This is mandatory!

What is the Pitch Canvas?

There are many possible structures for a pitch presentation depending on the framework. The option you choose must be always adapted to the target audience. A template should never be used directly. The Pitch Canvas is a tool to check the different items that should be included in a pitch so that it is possible to verify that all the critical elements are present. It is a reference for the development of a template. It was created by David Beckett and Geert van Vlijmen, with the design work done by Birgit Smit from Best 3 Minutes Presentation Services in Amsterdam, in 2016.

The Pitch Canvas©

An entrepreneurial brainstorming tool that helps you structure and visualise your pitch on one page.

Simple Statement of what change you and your product are making in the world.

A memorable one-sentence explanation of what you do for customers.

Pain (+ Gain)

What problem are you solving for your customers?
What does the pain result in?
Can you make the pain a human problem, that everyone can relate to?
How many people need this problem solved - market size?
Have you validated that people will pay to have it solved?

Product

As simply as possible: what does your product do for customers?
What opportunities do you provide for people to be faster, more cost-effective, more efficient, happier, safer?
How does it work?
How have you tested it with customers?
(Be sure not to let the product dominate the pitch.)

Product Demo

Live demo? (always risky, but powerful if it works..)
A screenflow movie of a working app convinces this is for real. Physical product convinces you can execute.
Screenshots are also OK, but can look like a mock-up - moving product on screen is better.
Can you show a real customer using it?

What's Unique

Technology/Relationships/Partnerships.
How do you help your customers get results differently to your competition, or alternatives?
Show you have researched the market and know what competition is out there.

Customer Traction

Success so far?
Pilot customers? Major brands?
Progression in users or downloads?
Customer reference quotes or movies?
PR coverage? Competition wins?
Use data and facts to strengthen your case.

Business Model

How do you get paid?
What's the opportunity for growth?
How can you scale beyond your current scope: new industries, territories, applications of partnerships and technology?

Investment

Have you invested money yourself?
Have you raised money so far?
How much are you looking for now?
What big next steps will you use the investment for?
What milestones will you reach with the money?
How many, and what type of investor are you looking for?
What expectations do you have of your investors, network, expertise?

Team

What relevant experience and skills does your team have that supports your story?
Brands worked for? Achievements? Sales success?
What binds you together as people and as entrepreneurs to fix this problem?
What's special about the character of your team, that will make you stand out and be memorable?

Call To Action and End Statement

Finish the pitch strongly with a clear request for the audience to take action - what is their first next step?

Why You?

NOTE: Why You? can show up in any part of the pitch.
Why do you care about solving this problem for your customers? How has your life been affected by this industry and business?
Why should your audience have confidence that you are driven to do what you promise, no matter what?

DESIGNED BY: Best3Minutes
Developed from an original idea by David Beckett

Best 3 Minutes

KEY IDEAS AND REFERENCES FOR MORE INFORMATION

- the option to use a template to develop a pitch depends on the framework but must be always a iterative process with as many version as needed
- a pitch master deck is a very useful tool to develop a good pitch – Investor Pitch Deck Template – www.slidebooks.com/products/investor-pitch-template

[1] Buccino, R. (2013). The Pitch Book: New Thinking for New Business.
[2] The Pitch Canvas. Version 7.8. (2016) http://msuhatch.com/wp-content/uploads/2016/11/pitch-outline.pdf [accessed in 2018 Jan. 20]

19

How to develop and implement the Business Case?

What is the flow for implementation of a Business Case?

Once we have a business case, what are the next steps? There are several actions that can be taken in parallel: (1) present the business case pitch and establish a financial framework; (2) consolidate the team; (3) start developing the business with clients. The business must be customer-centric and based on clients, but always supported by a team. The process is iterative and must have several intermediate validation points where the strategy and tactics might need to be adjusted. This is the key topic for the BCR Volume 2.

How to transform Leads into Prospects?

This is the most difficult priority in business development and with highest impact on short-term success. Customers decide quickly, move often, change their minds and shift their loyalty easily. Smart businesses make ongoing efforts to forge relationships with customers who match their ideal lead profile and convert those leads to prospects. Prospects are leads who show interest or potential to buy your products or services. First determine the best prospects from the leads you have generated through a ranking, considering the following parameters: (1) a need for your product or service; (2) the ability to make a decision to buy; (3) the ability to pay. This process is called qualifying your leads. Once you have qualified your leads, you may find that you have several prospects. Decide where to prioritize your efforts by assessing both the probability of closing the sale, and the value of the sale. Achieving success quickly is critical as it potentially generates a cascade effect with a 'me too' market response.

What is the business development framework, based on best practices?

There is a logical path from market opportunities to clients.

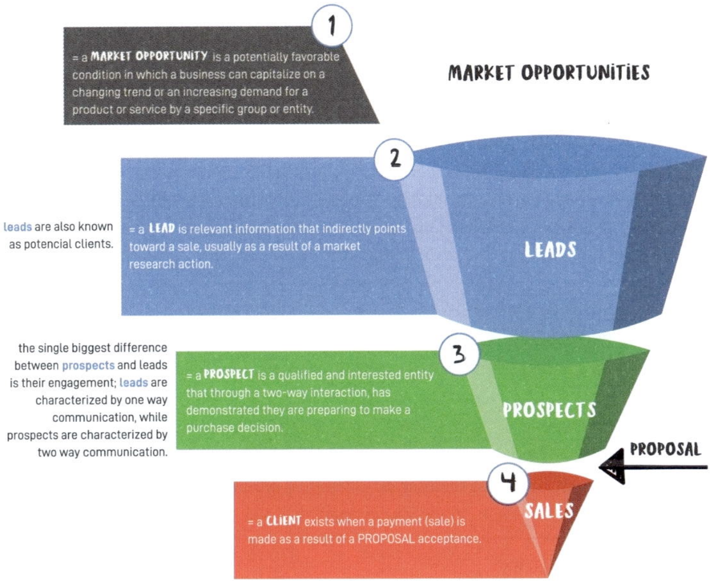

How to convert Prospects into Clients?

The 'best practices' when it comes to converting prospects into clients have been studied by many experts along many years and in different fields of activity. A possible way they can be summarized is as follows, for a 'services business':

1. Dialogue for Exploration

The heart of the selling conversation is exploring the prospective client's situation and challenges.

We want to ask a ⋆lot⋆ of questions to really understand clients':

Situation – What's happening now, what's working, details about how their business works.

Challenges – What's not working, what are their problems, what have they tried up to this point, and the future landscape.

This is the longest part of the selling conversation and requires about 75% or more of our time. Our aim is to really understand why this prospect needs our products or services. It is akin to a diagnosis. Without it, we cannot recommend a course of action. We can build a lot of trust during this conversation if we handle it well. We should be able to listen closely, go deep enough to discover the most pressing challenges and issues, and show, through various examples, that we can help them succeed.

2. Discussion for Possibilities

Once we understand our prospect's situation and challenges, we want to talk about the future. What objectives do they want to attain? We want to listen closely and really get what it is they want. And we need to be sure that this is something we can actually help them with. Then we want to feed this back in their own words. This part of the conversation might not take too long, but we need to go deep enough so they see a new future for themselves. Ultimately, prospects "buy the future" from us. And if this future is not compelling enough, they will not buy it.

3. Debate for Clarity

Next, we present our solution (service or program) that will help them achieve their goals. Note, that if we have sent (and they've read) some detailed information on our services, we don't need to tell them a lot. Normally we can confirm that most prospects have read the information on services very thoroughly. They mostly understand what we are offering and they may have a few questions to help them be crystal clear about how our services can help them. Once we've answered their final questions, we usually say: we are not asking the client, at this point, if they want to work with us. We are telling them that we want to work with them. But at no point are we really ⋆persuading or pushing⋆ our prospect to work with us.

4. Discussion for Commitment

Now it's time to ask if they think our services are right for them. There are a couple of ways to say it; it's really that simple. In a high percentage of cases, they will say yes. Closing doesn't need to be tricky or manipulative. And then we'll

ask, "Do you have any other questions?" If they don't know our fees yet, they'll usually ask, "What are the fees for your services or program?" And we'll answer in the next conversation.
5. Negotiation of Fees Sometimes a person will not answer the above question about the service or program being right for them until they know our fees. We want to know if there's a fit. If there isn't we won't even talk about the fees. We're done. But if they say it feels like a fit, then they've made a commitment at a certain level. And then it's easy to talk about fees. If they are not sure it's a fit, we can explore more about what they want and answer other questions they may have. We have already received a yes that they want to work with us. Now we are just confirming that they can afford it.
6. Call to Action Now that the client has agreed to work with us, we just need to finalize things. The final conversation gets them home and ready to start.

Source: adapted from Six Steps to Converting Prospects into Paying Clients (2017)

Most of the time products can be sold as services – depending on the business model – but services are very difficult (although not impossible) to sell as products. The 'sale' is the ultimate validation for a business and a key requirement before scale-up.

KEY IDEAS AND REFERENCES FOR MORE INFORMATION

- the conversion of leads into prospects and then into profitable clients is the main challenge of any business
- the use of reference definitions is critical so that all the organizations have the same framework to work in the same direction

[1] Saleh, K. & Shukairy, A. (2010). Conversion Optimization: The Art and Science of Converting Prospects to Customers.
[2] Middleton, R. (2017). Six Steps to Converting Prospects into Paying Clients – www.actionplan.com/blog/663-selling-steps [accessed in 2018 Jan. 20]

20

What is the role of the Business Case in transforming Ideas into Business?

What are the reasons to use the Business Case to develop a business idea?

The business case provides a clear definition of qualified information for validation and decision. It represents the minimum level of information that is generally necessary to evaluate a business. Some businesses can require less and some even require a complete and traditional 'business plan', depending also on who is doing the evaluation, and for what purpose. The Business Case is a compact source of information that can be summarized as:

The idea	All about the concept and value proposition
The clients	All about the market = clients and competitors – includes differentiation and market positioning
The team	All about implementation and how the team will execute. Includes the marketing approach
The trade	All about investment, costs, sales and key performance ratios and scenario-based performance

What is the role of the Business Case for entrepreneurs?

The business case can be used as the first step roadmap for implementation, but it starts being a simulation tool providing a qualified validation tool because it shows the big picture from idea to market. Entrepreneurs or business promoters can use the business case as a guide or a reference plan for implementation, providing a guarantee that there is alignment between the objectives and expected outcomes for the whole team involved. The business case must be a joint activity of all the core team. Being a compact document, it can easily be discussed in detail and changed according to the evolution of the business framework.

What is the role of the Business Case for stakeholders?

The business case is the heart of a project charter. More than just explaining the intent, value and end goal of the project, it should serve as a motivational tool to keep the team (and leadership) excited and engaged. The business case is a written document that validates the effort of the team that designed the whole project. From its goal statement to metrics, it must be well thought out and articulated, not just as a roadmap, but also as justification for the investment of the organization's time and resources. Therefore the business case – either directly or as a special external version (typically the BC is an internal document, mostly for the team) – can easily be transformed into a document for other stakeholders (after removing some personal information/details), to act as a reference tool for stakeholders and investors to follow the business.

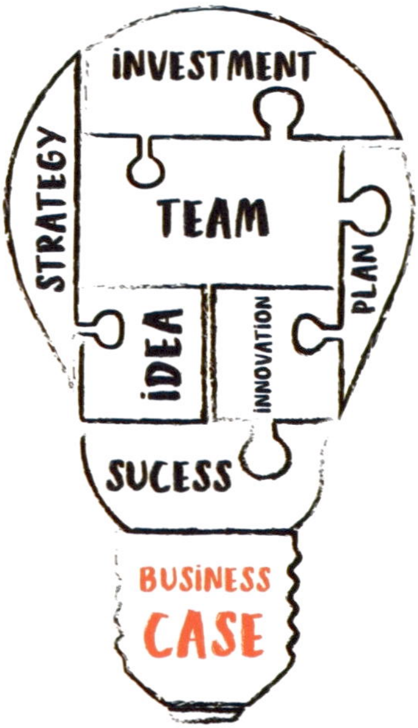

How do we validate the Business Case?

Once we have a business case, validating it requires going back to the beginning. There are several possible levels of validation. The first is self-validation, based on the core team's responses to a set of questions. These questions can be discussed in detail with consultants, business analysts and other external stakeholders. Complimentary validation tools can also be used to explore specific questions. However the ultimate market validation method will be through pre-market testing and the capacity to obtain the necessary resources (usually the financing). Very often, businesses pass all the validation stages

– including market validation – but still wind up unable to obtain the necessary financing. This means the team doesn't have the necessary skills to launch that specific business at that specific moment in time.

Most common 'self-validation' questions	Other (alternative) validation tools
Why do you want to start your business?	
Do you have experience in this sector?	The SWOT analysis – can be very subjective
Which qualities or skills make your team suitable?	
What is the value of your target market?	The PESTEL analysis – external focus
Is your market growing?	
Is it a competitive market?	The Market Research Plan – only the market issues
How will you promote the products or services?	
Will your customers need to make repeat purchases?	The Business Case itself
How will you stand out in your market?	
Do you need investment to start your business?	The Business Plan (more complex and time consuming)

What will be the future success criteria for a Business Case?

The success of a business case can be evaluated from two perspectives: (1) the originators of the business case and/or the entrepreneurs; and (2) the beneficiaries of the resulting business. The first question, in any case, is: success for who? The team/company or the beneficiaries? It is a response that depends pretty much on a combination of three factors: the alignment between the team, the idea, and the *momentum*.

It is critical to define from the start the expected outcomes for the different parties involved so that a realistic set of objectives can be shared by them all. If the success factors are known from the beginning they can be worked out during the course of the business development. A good example of this is that financing is a concern that must be developed throughout the development of the business. It is not possible to get a commitment from potential investors in the early stages but is possible to include this requirement in the development process and have the networking strategy ready when the 'window of opportunity' comes.

Why is the 'Business Case' approach being used beyond start up business?

It is common to hear start-ups talking about the 'business case', but it is also becoming common to see large companies using this tool to evaluate businesses at a department level. Universities are starting to use the 'business case' approach to evaluate business – including 'social business'. The scope of its applications range from departments in large companies to public services and non-governmental organizations. The business case concept is very appealing and interesting because it represents a major change of mindset from the complex requirement of a business plan to a 'simplified document' that can be potentially 'easier' to develop and present.

KEY IDEAS AND REFERENCES FOR MORE INFORMATION

- the business case development and validation is a process that creates the conditions to evolve from one idea to other
- failing to plan is planning to fail... the business case process allows for consistent business prototyping and validation

[1] Flynn, P. (2016). Will It Fly? How to Test Your Next Business Idea So You Don't Waste Your Time and Money.

[2] Levesque, R. (2015). Ask. Dunham Books.

21

Concluding remarks and Key ideas

It is possible to summarize the global mindset regarding the essentials of business development thus:

Businesses exist for clients (to satisfy a specific need or set of needs) ...and with 'no clients' ...there is no business, just an activity...

The team to promote the business is mandatory as without a Team there is no real business !

> Every business must be customer-centric and based on clients but supported by a team.

• There is a great business advantage if the possible paths, and common mistakes, are known in advance...

(Exploring the mistakes of others is smart and may bring new abilities and competences)

• It is possible to learn from best practices and obtain a competitive advantage.

To Think Big (global, international...), Act Small and Move Fast are key drivers for business development...

The 'force field' ideas that were presented over the previous pages can be described as follows:

The 'business evolution life-cycle', that predicts the future, helps to know what will happen in advance...
The 'understanding of the 'business motivations' helps to set a logical framework for decision-making...
The 'definition of a Mission, Vision, Values', helps to define a 'business DNA' and share a will...
The 'concept of master documents', helps to organize steps such as ideation and innovation...
The 'concept of creating a check-list', provides a better systematic approach to business development...
The 'Ikigai framework' offers a new vision for finding and developing teams...
The 'Canvas best practices' from the lean canvas, business model canvas and pitch canvas, are powerful tools...
The 'PESTLE and associated tools' show that there is more beyond the team and the clients...
The 'cascade analysis', starting with market validation and a focus on clients, brings a critical mindset...
The 'innovation process' is essential for success, because it brings value and provides differentiation
The 'systematic validation' is critical before action, but must be done when ideas are mature and after benchmarking
The 'business development' is an iterative process of disruptive moments followed by continuous improvements...

Following a question and answer approach it was possible to describe a possible roadmap from the Idea to the Business Case. At the same time, a consistent set of diverse knowledge about business development was introduced and presented, providing a learning platform. The proposed approach was tested over several years with several dozen entrepreneurs and MBA students, with very positive results.

Key concepts that are critical for the Business Case formulation

There are some definitions that are critical to formulate a modern business and to have a clear understanding about the complexities behind the business framework. There is no 'international set of standards' for business-related definitions but combining academic information and business best practices it is possible to provide a possible set of definitions that are usually considered:

need = something that someone (prospective client) wants or thinks that he/she wants

price = amount of money charged for a product or service, or the sum of the values that consumers exchange for the benefit of having or using a product or service

market = real or virtual place where the business-related exchanges happen
> market value = the currency value or quantity of all exchanges in a certain segment over a certain time

value proposition = a promise of value (benefit) to be delivered, communicated, and acknowledged
= a belief from the customer about how value will be delivered, experienced and acquired
= a business or marketing statement used to summarize why a consumer and/or client should buy a product or use a service
> applies to an entire organization, or parts, or customer accounts, or products or services

differentiation = blend of options related to cost, innovation and / or customer relationships

positioning = the place that a brand occupies in the mind of the customer and how it is distinguished from competitor options

business model = how an organization creates, delivers, and captures value

competitor = the organizations that provide an answer to the same need

competitive advantage = the attributes that allow an organization to outperform its competitors
> such as access to natural resources, energy sources, skilled labor, geographical location, entry barriers, access to new technology, etc.

business value chain = set of steps from production, distribution, retail to the consumer (a good example is the "farm to fork" process)

momentum = the complex mix of 'being at the right time' where a set of events or opportunities happen

Finally, one of the more frequent questions about definitions related to business development:

• **What is the difference between Client, Customer and Consumer?**

Client = pays for or exchanges products or services for direct use or to pass on to third parties for money or other forms of pay

Customer = the same as client
= however typically (but not always) the customer buys goods or services from a business (rather than an individual or group of professionals); the wording 'customer' is used for B2B.

Consumer = user or end beneficiary of a product or service
> sometimes they are the client (they pay for the product or service) but it is possible too that they get it from others or even for free.

Vol. 2 – The BCR - how to Implement the Business Case: the execution challenge

This volume describes **how to use the Business Case as a tool for execution**. It is recommended that the Business Case is implemented through execution programmes or plans with the support of checklists. The programmes refer to the continuous activity functions of a company as people management – and plans refer to time-related activities as the 'go-to-market plan'. The programmes are inspired by accumulated knowledge from Project Management as in the PMBOK (Project Management Book of Knowledge). Depending on the nature of the business, different approaches might be required but the general logic is always the same, because for every business, its reason to exist is related to its clients. The management of the competitive environment and of the available resources (including financing) is the driving force behind the process of satisfying clients' needs. Implementation, based on the Business Case tool, often involves adding execution programmes as annexes to the Business Case, so that there is a combined process and integrated vision. Key ideas: Customer centric, PMBOK and Best practices.

Vol. 2 – How to implement the Business Case: the execution challenge

Introduction and expected results
Why an algorithmic logic?

1. *What is the The Business Case Check-List?*
2. *How to manage time to develop a business idea?*
3. *How to define management objectives and management priorities?*
4. *What are the best practices in the implementation of a business case?*
5. *What is the role of corporate DNA in business development?*
6. *Why a business must be customer centric and focused in value creation?* Why must a business be customer-centric and focused on value creation?
7. *What are Management Programmes and Management Plans?*
8. *What are the key success factors in go-to-market?*
9. *How to implement and use the balanced score cards as a management tool?*
10. *How to use the routine management maps?*
11. *What is the role of 'business intelligence' in the smart decision process?*
12. *How to develop continuous benchmarking process and market analysis?*
13. *How to develop competitor and client profiling? For segmentation and positioning?*
14. *How to develop the marketing programme? And the related communication plan?*
15. *How to develop a commercial plan?*
16. *What is the role of networking in business development?*

17. *How to develop a partnership programme with suppliers, stakeholders and even competitors?*
18. *How to develop costing and budgeting?*
19. *What is the relevance of risk analysis management ?*
20. *Why failing to plan is planning to fail?*
21. *Concluding remarks*

Vol. 3 – The BCR - how to expand the Business Case for business growth and avoid pitfalls

This volume describes **how to evolve from a start up to higher levels of business development** as a scaler or a scale-up. It explains the challenges which prevent a company from scaling up, as well as the opportunities for doing so. The book also evaluates best practices for business longevity, using an analysis of centennial companies. It assesses the best practice strategies of star companies that inspire entrepreneurs. Methodologies to avoid common difficulties – and avoid failure – are discussed in detail. The most relevant do's and don'ts are unveiled, providing a unique set of options and paths that can lead to better business results. Containing easy-to-understand and critically organized information, the volume provides invaluable knowledge gleaned from the experience of others, which will help you make better decisions. Key ideas: Extended team, Market, Resources.

Vol. 3 – How to expand the Business Case for business growth and avoid pitfall

Introduction and expected results
Why an algorithmic logic?

1. *What is the 'life cycle' of companies?*
2. *What is the role of strategy in business expansion?*
3. *How to develop a strategic programme for business expansion?*
4. *What are the best practices for raising money for a developing business?*
5. *How are investment rounds organised and how to use them?*
6. *How to deal with and manage investors?*
7. *Why do some companies grow faster?*
8. *Why do some companies live longer?*
9. *What is the evolution process from startup, scaleup and scaler?*
10. *What are gazelle companies? And what can we learn from them?*
11. *What are unicorn companies? And what we learn from them?*
12. *What are the common characteristics of inspiring and fast growing companies?*
13. *What are the most common business failure factors?*
14. *How can disruptive business models be adapted for any business?*
15. *How to combine exports with international business development?*
16. *What are the drivers for the International Marketing Plan?*
17. *How to use 'value chain analysis' for business development?*
18. *What are the main challenges for developing business?*
19. *What are the main business management and business strategy mistakes? How to avoid them?*
20. *How to sell a business?*
21. *Concluding remarks*